FULLY DEVOTED

ONE CHURCH'S JOURNEY WITH GOD

Dedicated to the people of Willow Creek Community Church,
from its earliest days, across the years, and into the future:
You have invited God into your stories with open hearts and joyful sacrifice.
Thank you for sharing some of those stories in this book.
As we eagerly anticipate the next chapters of our lives together,
may we be unwavering in our full devotion to Jesus Christ.

CONTENTS

A MESSAGE
FROM SENIOR PASTOR BILL HYBELS

To my Willow Creek family,

It's hard to believe 35 years have passed since October 12, 1975, when we first swung open the doors to the old Willow Creek Theatre in Palatine, admitting 125 or so brave people for our very first Willow Creek service. The Woody Allen film *Everything You Always Wanted to Know About Sex, But Were Afraid to Ask* blared across the theatre marquee that morning, making the place seem all the less likely to be somewhere God would show up.

But show up He did. And He has continued to show up in each of our lives, through thick and thin, failure and heartache, celebration and victory. For 35 years, He has used you, the Willow Creek family—a rugged band of believers fully devoted to Christ—to be a light on the hill, a place of belonging, and a welcoming front door to those far from God.

When we first started Willow, I had the strong sense that I wanted to spend my life in just one church, serving the people there, doing life together with them. I remember thinking, "This isn't a five-year challenge. It may take a lifetime for me to grow up to become a good leader, and it may take a lifetime for a church to become an Acts 2 community. I would like to give the major portion of my life to the same church, if God would have me do that and if the congregation would be open to it."

Whether by Spirit-led inspiration or stalled inertia, you have seen fit to have me continue in this role these past many years. What a privilege to watch our church grow to become the kind of life-changing, kingdom-bringing, authentic biblical community we find described in Acts 2:42–47. (No comment on how I've done at becoming that "good leader." Hopefully, I've still got time!)

Much has changed since 1975. Polyester pantsuits, puka shells, and the Ford Pinto have been replaced by skinny jeans, body piercings, and the Toyota Prius. But for me, some things never change.

I am still moved to tears when a person who is far from God has a redemptive encounter with Christ that changes him or her forever. In the early days, Baptisms produced tremendous joy in my life, and in recent years, this has only grown. Perhaps age and experience have given me a deeper understanding of and appreciation for what happens when a person surrenders his or her life to a loving God and enters the waters of Baptism.

I still love seeing someone get gripped by the power of the Holy Spirit and watching their character gradually conform to the image of Christ. I love seeing someone who was greedy become generous, and someone who was hateful become radically loving. I love seeing someone prejudiced become inclusive, someone insular become globally minded. It is only the power of God that brings about those kinds of radical life transformations. I celebrate every one of those changes in peoples' fundamental attitudes and behaviors, and I celebrate them in myself when I sense God has nudged my own character ever so slightly in the direction of Christ.

I still get really excited when someone finds their new 'cause,' when they get tapped on the shoulder by the Holy Spirit and called to pursue a 'good work' with passion and diligence. It's a never-ending point of fascination to see who gets prompted by what cause, and to watch them get increasingly fired up as they become difference makers in God's kingdom.

But perhaps the biggest thing that remains unchanged in me since the earliest days at Willow is the deep gratitude I feel to be sharing this journey with a team of friends. Since the day Lynne and I launched the church with three other couples (Tim and Erin Vanden Bos, Scott and Laurie Pederson, and Joel and Cathy Jager), I have enjoyed the privilege of serving alongside a team of friends—lifelong friends as well as new—a team consistently made stronger by the unique gifts of each person.

Many years ago, I was preparing a talk for a conference on the subject of leadership styles. Sitting in a booth at a cheap diner, tablet and pen in hand, I scratched out a dozen or so leadership styles that different leaders employ. When I began to write about *team leadership*, immediately I found myself choking up and getting uncharacteristically misty. Wiping my eyes with my paper napkin, I pondered why this particular leadership style struck such an emotional chord with me. And I realized it's because this has been *my* leadership story. Since Willow began, I've experienced the privilege of being part of a team where every person's gifts are vital to the whole, where men and women alike bring their "A" game to the table and we work together as a community for the common purpose of making an eternal difference in God's kingdom.

As you read through these pages and see the hand of God at work in the stories of His people, notice as I have, how consistently and dramatically He works in peoples' lives through the power of a team. Reflect on your own life and identify the team of people God has placed around you to play a role in your story. And take note of how He's used you to be part of someone else's story. This is the power of community lived out through the stories of the individuals and families who, together, make up the church of Jesus Christ.

It never ceases to amaze me, when I take the time to look in the rearview mirror of my life, to see how faithfully present, available, trustworthy, and powerful God has been. It is no wonder the psalmist was compelled to tell of His might.

I will tell everyone about Your righteousness. All day long I will proclaim Your saving power, though I am not skilled with words. I will praise Your mighty deeds, O Sovereign Lord. I will tell everyone that You alone are just.
—Psalm 71:15–16 (NLT)

When I look at all God has done in each of our lives and as a community of Christ followers called Willow Creek, I am humbled and speechless. Only God. Only God could have crafted a story such as ours. Only the God of the universe could take a bunch of polyester-wearing kids and—over the years in with His strength and direction—give us the privilege of playing a role in building His kingdom.

Only God.

Bill Hybels
October, 2010

They devoted themselves to the **apostles' teaching** and to the fellowship, to the breaking of bread and to prayer. Everyone was filled with awe, and many wonders and miraculous signs were done by the apostles. **All the believers were together** and **had everything in common.** Selling their possessions and goods, **they gave to anyone as he had need.** Every day they **continued to meet together** in the temple courts. They broke bread in their homes and ate together with glad and sincere hearts, praising God and enjoying the favor of all the people. And **the Lord added** to their number daily those who were being saved.

—Acts 2:42–47

New Testament professor
Dr. Gilbert Bilezikian challenges college student Bill
Hybels with the dream of
creating an Acts 2 church.

01 FULLY LOVED

01

FULLY LOVED
PEOPLE MATTER TO GOD

The Power of Doing Life Together

Perhaps you've felt it at your high school reunion—that warm, familiar feeling of being among old friends, retelling tales of how your team beat the rival school for the district championship, or how you survived Pre-Algebra/Trig with impossible Mr. Franklin, or the daring—and *relatively* harmless—senior prank you pulled off without a hitch.

The teens and leaders of the Son City youth group in Park Ridge form the kind of biblical community described in Acts 2, loving one another with an authentic Christ-centered love. This community becomes the foundation of Willow Creek Community Church.

Or perhaps you've felt it—*experienced it*—at a family gathering. The house is crowded with aunts, uncles, grandparents, cousins—some you know and love, and others you only know through occasional gatherings such as this. Plates piled high with burgers and potato salad slowly empty as loved ones mingle together, sharing food, laughter, quiet conversation.

And then the stories begin. "Remember when…?" someone says. Kids' ears perk up and they gather around.

"Do you remember the time we took that trip to…?"

"Tell about that Christmas when…."

"Tell us again about the night Dad was born."

Many have heard these stories before—and it only heightens the telling. But there are always new folks being enfolded into the circle, people who have not heard. Sons-in-law, daughters-in-law who wonder with widened eyes, "Who is this family I've married into?" And there are the children—the most enthusiastic lovers of a good tale—who were too young last time you gathered to remember the stories. Now they soak up every word, longing to know—and be part of—a community bigger than themselves.

Something powerful happens when a community of friends and family gathers to tell their stories. It's not about the stories themselves, really. It's about the rolling years of history, the shared experience, the common bond of doing life together. But the telling of these stories defines the community, honors each member, and creates a feeling of belonging that is palpable, sturdy, resilient.

As Christ followers, we are invited into this kind of community—and more. With God before us and at our side, we do life together—celebrating, grieving, laughing, crying, praising, praying—united during times both of heartbreak and of joy.

It's a bond we share with our spiritual ancestors. It's the bond of Noah and his family, sharing tight quarters and rainy nights for 40 days and nights. It's the bond of the nation of Israel, sharing tents and manna throughout a 40-year camping trip. It's the bond of a band of disciples, following a controversial Rabbi from village to village—dusty roads, worn-out sandals, and hungry crowds to feed. It's the bond of the early church, sharing everything they had, reaching out to those beyond their circle, and together tasting a bit of God's "kingdom come, on earth as it is in heaven."[1]

Since 1975, it's been the bond shared by a group of friends known today as Willow Creek Community Church. For the past 35 years, this ever-expanding circle of believers has witnessed time and again God's hand at work in their lives. If you count yourself among Willow's family of Christ followers, then these 35 years are part of your spiritual heritage, a story from your "family reunion." You play a role here. You are part of the story God has written through this church, this body of Christ called Willow Creek.

And if you belong to a band of Christ followers beyond the circle of Willow Creek, you will likely spot yourself and your church reflected in the pages to come—in the common values and stories of God's active and loving hand in the lives of those who, like you, follow Christ.

And if you are exploring what it means to follow Christ, we invite you to look beyond the specifics of these stories, beyond the earnest but sometimes faulty ways we live out God's activity, and look into the eyes and heart of a God who always gives His children only His best. At every turn, He is present, persistent, extending His love to you and inviting you into a larger family, a community beyond yourself. We invite you to do some rigorous, intelligent exploring. Perhaps you will conclude as we have, that His circle is one worth joining.

Only God...
The specifics of the stories change—and will continue to change through the years—but the common denominator remains the same: God. The headline story is not about the particular experience or activity of any one individual or church, but rather about the ongoing work of God. He accompanies us through every turn in the road, His comforting presence is felt in every wound or failure, and His thumbprint marks every victory.

It's a common phrase heard around Willow: "Only God." Underlying the unspoken part of this expression is: "Only our amazing God could have ...

"... helped a young, inexperienced bunch of leaders and teenagers launch and lead the church that has become Willow Creek."

"... provided the resources needed to sustain a long-term ministry endeavor."

"... healed the wounds we've inflicted upon one another at various times, through our own immaturity and sinfulness."

"... turned a one-time meeting of 26 pastors into an international organization reaching 1.5 million pastors and church leaders.

"... protected and encouraged us when criticism or attack came our way."

"... guided us toward decisions that turned out to be exactly what were needed, though we couldn't have known it at the time."

"... opened the hearts of His people to bridge the racial divide with such commitment and oneness."

"... prompted His people to give their time, resources, and hearts to ease the pain of those struggling against AIDS, poverty, hunger, thirst, disease, injustice."

"... nurtured a vibrant Spanish-speaking community within our congregation."

Telling the story of God's activity in our lives is nothing new. Throughout Scripture, God's people have been compelled by their love for Him to tell His story. The psalmist proclaims:

"One generation will commend Your works to another; they will tell of Your mighty acts." —Psalm 145:4

"Praise Him for His acts of power; praise Him for His surpassing greatness. " —Psalm 150:2

One of the Apostle Peter's first actions in the book of Acts is his powerful re-telling of God's activity among the nation of Israel, from Abraham through the resurrection of Jesus.[2]

Stephen's last words before being stoned to death recount the mighty works of God through His people.[3]

The author of Hebrews tells story after story of God's activity through "the great cloud of witnesses" [4]—the spiritual ancestors who went before us.

At this milestone anniversary of Willow Creek Community Church, we too desire to put into words the story of God's impact on our lives, to honor Him and place any glory or credit where it is properly due: at His feet alone.

How It All Began

It was fall of 1972. In a college classroom in Deerfield, Illinois, 20-year-old Bill Hybels sat captivated by the picture his New Testament professor painted of the early church as described in Acts chapter 2. In his thick French accent,

Dr. Gilbert Bilezikian spoke passionately about a community of believers who loved each other with a radical kind of love, who took off their masks and shared their lives with one another, who laughed and cried and prayed and sang and served together in authentic Christian fellowship.

Dr. B's vision resonated deep in Bill's soul. "He was describing the kind of church I wanted to invite my friends to," Bill says, "a church where people passionately lived out the love of God in tangible, authentic ways. I was struck to the core by the beauty of that picture." Dr. B ended class that day with a challenge: Could this Acts 2 church exist again today?

"I left his classroom and went out to my car, put my head on the steering wheel, and cried," Bill says. "The dream of being part of such a church had taken root."

At the time, Bill and some friends were leading a high school youth group in Park Ridge, Illinois. As they began to apply the Acts 2 principles taught by Dr. B, the ministry exploded.

"We were shocked," says Bill. "Kids were coming to faith in Christ, their lives were being transformed, and they were loving one another with the kind of unconditional love you see described in Acts chapter 2.

"In the months that followed, Dr. B and I had many conversations. One in particular, I will never forget. We were sitting under a towering tree in his backyard.

"'These teachings of the early church are straight from the Bible, correct?' I asked. 'Yes,' Dr. B said. 'So they are *universal* truths about God's design for His followers?' I asked. 'Yes,' he repeated. 'Then couldn't they be applied—not just to students—but to adults, families, a whole church?' I asked. 'Absolutely they could,' Dr. B told me. And I knew at that point God was inviting me to follow His lead in helping to build such a church."

Throughout the past three-and-a-half decades, Bill and the Elders and leaders of Willow Creek have continued, as best they understand, to follow God's lead in building an Acts 2 church. Key themes, taken directly from that Scripture passage in Acts, have transcended individual leaders, ministries, and eras, and have woven themselves deeply into the fabric of who Willow Creek is as a church:

They devoted themselves to the apostles' teaching and to the fellowship, to the breaking of bread and to prayer. Everyone was filled with awe, and many wonders and miraculous signs were done by the apostles. —Acts 2:42–43

The devotion of the Acts 2 believers to consistent teaching, fellowship, Communion, and prayer has provided Willow Creek's leadership with a clear pattern for *discipleship*—the process of becoming more like Christ.

All the believers were together…   —Acts 2:44a

In reading that "*all* the believers were together," Bill and the leaders found a challenge to engage with the church *beyond* our doors—the global church—across the country and eventually across the world.

[They] had everything in common. Selling their possessions and goods, they gave to anyone as he had need.   —Acts 2:44b–45

The early believers' willingness to sell their possessions and give to anyone as they had need inspired acts of *compassion* to be a top Willow Creek priority.

Every day they continued to meet together in the temple courts. They broke bread in their homes and ate together with glad and sincere hearts, praising God and enjoying the favor of all the people.   —Acts 2:46–47a

Their commitment to meeting together in the temple, sharing meals in homes, and praising God together modeled the value of *community*.

And the Lord added to their number daily those who were being saved.
                                                          —Acts 2:47b

The continual influx of new followers of Jesus into the early church affirmed the role of *evangelism* as a natural and vital element of the local church. These transcendent themes modeled by the early church and recorded in Acts 2 have been—and continue to be—the cornerstones of Willow Creek's singular mission.

The Mission

In launching this fledgling suburban church, Bill and his friends were dead serious about one thing: they wanted their friends who were far from God to know Christ. Willow Creek was founded on this core belief: **"People matter to God; therefore they matter to us."** People matter so deeply to our loving God that He bridged the unfathomable chasm between His holiness and our sin-stained humanity through the death and resurrection of His Son Jesus Christ. This mission is driven by our passion for people to experience the love and forgiveness of God, available only through Jesus Christ. Simply stated, **Willow Creek's mission is to turn irreligious people into fully devoted followers of Jesus Christ.**

The Methods

The mission is unchanging; but the *methods* for achieving the mission are not. How Willow implements its mission—the methods and ministries utilized to turn irreligious people into fully devoted Christ followers—has changed continually over the years. Sociological shifts in our culture, staffing changes, new data from the Reveal™ study,[5] trial and error, and the simple following of the Holy Spirit's whisper have all been reasons why methods at Willow change—and will continue to change in the future.

"Willow Creek has always been open to a sense of constant movement," says Bill. "Not a restless addiction to change for change's sake, but an ongoing, rolling, vital unfolding of the Holy Spirit's plan. Following Him means saying yes to unexpected turns and surprise events. **The methods, year upon year, have changed, but whatever the methods, Willow Creek's mission has remained the same.**"

In the coming pages, we'll unpack each of these transcendent themes from Acts 2 and examine how they've been lived out at Willow Creek. We'll hear stories of how God impacted peoples' lives "back in the day" and throughout the past 35 years. And we'll take a look at how He's continuing to impact peoples' lives today—and beyond.

02 FULLY COMMITTED

At Willow Creek's 20th anniversary celebration, held in the United Center in Chicago, every guest is given a small flashlight. During one point in the service, Teaching Pastor Nancy Beach asks, "If you or someone in your family has come to faith in Christ through the people or ministries of Willow Creek, please turn on your lights." There is a momentary pause, and then the darkened arena lights up like a constellation, each point of light representing a life changed by Christ. At that moment, it is crystal clear—all the work, all the sacrifice, all the prayer, all the heartaches had been worth it: God had worked thousands of miracles over the last 20 years."

"Even the most seasoned Willow staff member was floored by the flood of light that filled the room," Nancy recalls. "The power of God to transform a human life will never cease to bring wonder." Lower left corner: Bill Hybels' mentor and a founding Willow Creek Elder, Dr. Gilbert Bilezikian takes in the tangible expression of God's activity in peoples' lives.

02
FULLY COMMITTED
EVANGELISM

"In 1988, I was in a bad spot. My marriage was in trouble and I was filled with discouragement about the state of my life. Then a friend invited me to Willow," says Donna.[6] "Bill delivered the gospel message and I accepted Christ into my life. Christ changed my life and saved my marriage."

otooo

Tony[7] relates: "I was born and raised Catholic, but in my late teens, church became less a priority. In 1993, my girlfriend (now my wife), Kimberly invited me to start attending Willow with her. I'll never forget the church service; about a year later, when Greg Ferguson sang, "A Place to Call Home," I accepted Christ and I have never been the same since. The day I was baptized, Greg Ferguson was again part of the worship band, which felt like an extra reminder of God's love on such a celebratory day. Kimberly and I have been married 17 years and have two beautiful daughters who are learning about Jesus every week in Promiseland."

otooo

Allison's[8] journey toward a relationship with Christ began as soon as she was born: "My parents started looking for a church once they had me," she says. "They stumbled upon Willow Creek and became believers here. So from my youngest days, I grew up in Promiseland, Sonlight [now Elevate], and Student Impact—awesome ministries for kids and students. I had caring small group leaders investing in me from the time I was a small child, which laid a solid foundation for my faith. Today, I'm 28 and about to move overseas long-term to reach out to refugees. I don't think I'd be ready to do this unless I'd received such great discipleship and guidance from so many volunteers at Willow over the course of my lifetime."

otooo

Shane Farmer, director of Willow Creek's Student Impact high school ministry, describes God's activity at a recent summer event: "This past July at Sandblast, our summer camp for students, we opened up 65 scholarship spots specifically for kids who had never been to a church before. Our camp speaker told his story of faith in Christ, and it hit home with our kids. Forty-nine kids received Jesus into their lives, and more than 700 students recommitted their lives to Him. The movement of the Spirit of God that night was palpable, and we are still feeling the ripple effects."

otooo

Krista's[9] story began more than two decades ago. "Here is the domino effect of inviting just one co-worker to church," she says. "In 1987, my mom was invited by a co-worker to a Willow Creek service. At the time, she was a newly single mom of three almost-teen kids—all heading for trouble. Because of that one invitation and a powerful drama sketch in the service that day, my mom eventually accepted Christ. Today, she is a Christian, along with all of her kids, her parents, all of her siblings and their spouses, her son-in-law and her grandkids, who now attend Promiseland. Mom invited one of her friends— also a single mom—and her five kids to Willow, and they have all given their lives to Christ. Now friends of my kids are coming with them to Promiseland where they are learning about God's love for them.

"All these lives have been forever changed because *one* bold co-worker invited my mom to church!" Krista says. "So, who are you thinking about asking? Just think—what if you *don't* ask? Our entire family and future generations depended upon that one invitation!"

"Elevate is an energy charged, age-relevant place where junior high students can bring their friends, knowing they will have fun, feel comfortable, and have a meaningful encounter with God."

Willow Creek—founded by a youth group and its leaders—knows the power of God when unleashed through high school students. Student Impact is fervent in its role of introducing teens to Jesus Christ and helping them develop an ever-deepening relationship with Him.

"Promiseland volunteers create a safe, fun experience where children— infants through grade 5—hear foundational truths of Scripture and learn to apply them to everyday life," says Pat Cimo, Promiseland director.

"Willow has been such an integral part of my family," Sandy[10] says, "from rais-ing our four daughters to be followers of Christ to the incredible marriage my husband and I enjoy because we've been equipped to reflect God at the center of our relationship. For years, I have prayed for my extended family to experience this same kind of relationship with God. Recently, my sister began attending Willow Creek North Shore. She committed her life to Christ, and she decided to get baptized this summer with her North Shore community. Standing on the shore of Lake Michigan, my family and I celebrated all God has done in her life—and ours."

otooo

Michelle[11] committed her life to Christ through a little sweat equity: "This spring, a team of Blitz Build volunteers from Willow Creek helped me build a house through Habitat for Humanity," she says. "Their love for God was plainly visible, and their hard work at helping someone they didn't even know made an impression. During the project, I talked with the volunteers about affirming my faith in Jesus through Baptism, and in June, I was baptized by some of the guys who hammered nails in my house. These carpenters led me to *the* carpenter—Jesus—and my life will never be the same."

otooo

Andy's[12] journey toward Christ was both personal and intellectual: "When I turned 38, that was the age my father was when he died, and it made me think, 'What if after this body dies, we still exist?' I started attending Willow Creek—mostly to appease my brother-in-law, if I were totally honest. But eventually, I joined a seeker small group. It was a safe place to ask tough questions, to raise objections. As I see it, my journey to faith in Jesus Christ was a series of hurdles. One by one, my questions were answered, my objec-tions were satisfied. I reached a point where I realized it would require more faith on my part to be an atheist than it would to become a Christian. There are good answers out there; there are solid reasons to believe. But intellec-tual investigation can only take you so far. In the end, the final step is a step of faith. I took that step, and have never looked back."

otooo

"I arrived at Willow through the 'back door' of Divorce Recovery," says Deb,[13] "and through those people who'd once been where I was now, I found hope that a real Jesus could exist. I began attending Willow's weekend services, came to faith in Christ, and in 2000, I was baptized. I found my faith because of the hope I found in Divorce Recovery."

José Fidel and Maribel's[14] pathway to God began on a 1989 airline flight home to Caracas, Venezuela. In a seat near them sat Mexican rock guitarist Hector Hermosillo and his brother Heriberto, well-known musicians for Mexico's leading musician, Luis Miguel.

"They invited us to their concert in Caracas," Maribel recalls. "My sister and I really enjoyed the concert, and my husband took a photo of us with Hector, to show our friends."

Fast-forward 17 years. Maribel and José Fidel are now living the Northwest Suburbs of Chicagoland, and José Fidel is an actuary for an international marketing company based in Chicago.

"We were from Venezuela, and both of us were raised in the Catholic church," José Fidel says. "But we were not happy at the church we were attending."

"One day, I was having lunch with a girlfriend," says Maribel, "and I asked her if she knew a good church with a Spanish-language service. She recommended Casa de Luz—and its pastor, Hector Hermosillo! 'The *musician?!*' I asked. 'Yes,' she told me. I was shocked. Hector had become a Christian and was now a pastor at Willow Creek. I went home and told my husband. We were very curious to see what had happened in Hector's life in the years since we'd met him on the airplane."

"Long story short," says José Fidel, "we came to Casa de Luz, loved it, and just kept coming back. It's been four years now, and we have rarely missed a Sunday. We accepted the Lord Jesus Christ as our Savior, and Hector baptized us in Willow's lake in 2007. Our children were baptized one year later. Today, we help out in Casa's Baptism ministry, lead a small group, and do some teaching for Casa. Our son José, 19, serves on Casa's production team and leads an Elevate small group; our daughter, Anabell, 16, also serves on Casa's production team. We enjoy volunteering our bilingual skills to help translate materials for Casa from English to Spanish. God has been so good to us. We are so grateful for His hand on our lives. Our family will never be the same, and all because of a 'random' trip to Venezuela in 1989. An amazing coincidence—or, as our Pastor Hector calls it, a 'God-cidence.' All the glory be to God."

Willow Creek holds several Baptism services throughout the year, including the annual Baptism in Willow's lake each June. In 2009, 1,682 people declared their faith in Jesus Christ, acknowledging His forgiveness of their sins, and celebrating their new life in Him by entering the waters of Baptism.

My God is mighty to save, He is mighty to save

... And the Lord added to their number daily those who were being saved.

—Acts 2:47

"What I love about the closing of that passage in Acts 2," says Bill Hybels, "is that it puts emphasis where it rightly belongs: 'And the *Lord* added to their number... .' Whenever someone is reconciled to God, it is always a result of the Holy Spirit at work—perhaps using our human efforts at representing Jesus Christ clearly and in an understandable way—but in the end, it is God and God alone who adds to the number."

BACK IN THE DAY

Since its earliest days, this Acts 2 description of God's redemptive work through the ministry of the early church has been the heartbeat of Willow.

"Throughout Scripture, we see a consistent picture of God's heart toward humankind," Bill says. "God is not passive. He doesn't sit around waiting for people to eventually stumble across Him. He is an activator, breaking down barriers and leveraging circumstances so we can recognize Him and respond to His love for us. One of the most dramatic images of God's initiative toward humankind is found in Jesus' description of God as the loving father in the parable of the lost son. In short, a self-absorbed son asks his dad to hand over his share of the inheritance early. The son pockets the cash, takes off, and squanders every last dime on wild living. Hungry and alone, he finally comes to his senses:

I will set out and go back to my father and say to him: "Father, I have sinned against heaven and against you. I am no longer worthy to be called your son; make me like one of your hired men." So he got up and went to his father.

But while he was still a long way off, his father saw him and was filled with compassion for him; he ran to his son, threw his arms around him and kissed him.

The son said to him, "Father, I have sinned against heaven and against you. I am no longer worthy to be called your son."

But the father said to his servants, "Quick! Bring the best robe and put it on him. Put a ring on his finger and sandals on his feet. Bring the fattened calf and kill it. Let's have a feast and celebrate. For this son of mine was dead and is alive again; he was lost and is found." So they began to celebrate.

—Luke 15: 18–24

"Just as the father in this story ran to meet his son, God runs to meet us," Bill says. "And in those early days of the Son City youth group and the theater, we were passionate about communicating that same love toward our friends—'running' to meet the people God brought our way. It is still this way at Willow today. We are committed to removing any cultural or generational barriers that would keep people at arms' length from the heavenly Father who runs to meet them, welcoming them into His outstretched arms."

Back in 1972, Bill Hybels and a handful of twenty-something leaders were committed to seeing young people come to faith in Christ, and were up to their eyeballs in serving and leading Son City, a church youth group in Park Ridge, Illinois. Bill's wife, Lynne recalls:

"The youth group … seemed like a page straight from the book of Acts. God was doing something real in that little group of high schoolers. [They] were suddenly charged with the kind of spiritual electricity I had read about in the Bible, but never seen. And together they formed a community of love that would eventually prove irresistible to hundreds of local unchurched students—and to me. … I felt as if I had fallen into a miracle."[15]

"A song we often sang during worship back then," says Bill, "is 'Two Hands,'[16] by the Christian rock group Love Song. Its chorus beautifully summed up how our little community was living out God's call on their lives:

'Accept Him with your whole heart, and use you own two hands. With one reach out to Jesus, and with the other, bring a friend.'

A Safe Place for a Dangerous Message
"One of the top priorities of our Son City leaders," says Lynne, "was to create events where kids could invite their friends who were far from God. Bill and the team planned weekly outreach services that were creative, energetic, contemporary, practical—and absolutely biblical. These events provided a safe place for kids with no church background to hear the dangerous, life-changing message of Jesus Christ."[17]

With clear leading from God to use the Acts 2 principles they had fleshed out in youth ministry to start a ministry for adults, Hybels and the Son City leaders began planning.

"We were just a bunch of kids who didn't know what we were doing," Bill says, "but we were dead serious about one thing: We wanted our friends to know Christ. Lots of people our age thought church was irrelevant or—worse—boring. The church I grew up in was a far cry from the church we sensed God leading us to build. I will be forever grateful for the solid values and doctrinal teaching I received in that church as a child. But to anyone but the already convinced, the average church service didn't seem like a 'normal' experience. We wanted to craft an experience that felt normal to someone who had never been to church. We wanted the music to sound like normal music, the drama sketches and media presentations to portray real-life experience, and the biblical messages to provide relevant, practical application that an average person would get. We sought to create a church service people would want to come to so they could hear the most important message on earth—the gospel of Jesus. We had no money, so we went door-to-door selling tomatoes to raise enough money for sound equipment. We rented a run-down movie theater in Palatine, Illinois. And that's the illustrious beginning of Willow Creek."

On a brisk autumn Sunday—October 12, 1975—the doors to the Willow Creek Theatre opened and 125 or so people gathered for the first Willow Creek service. Utilizing drama, multi-media presentations, contemporary music, and teachings from Scripture, Bill and the team brought the message of Jesus Christ to their friends in a way they could understand.

"This style of church service is more common now, but back then, it was a foreign concept in most churches," Bill says. "But God used it. The Holy Spirit moved, people responded to God, and the church grew."

Drama in Church?

One unique component of Son City and those early Willow Creek services was the use of drama to help set the stage for the message.

"The only 'church drama' I'd ever experienced growing up," Bill says, "was if a vocalist forgot the words to her solo or someone accidentally dropped a Communion tray. So when a 15-year-old girl named Nancy suggested we use drama in Son City to get kids thinking about the topic, I stared at her blankly—and promptly put her in charge."

That teenage girl was Nancy (Moore) Beach, and saying yes to Nancy eventually led to local churches all over the world being inspired to utilize the arts to help impact people with the message of Jesus Christ.

"Nancy began crafting and directing dramas to set the stage for whatever Scripture passage I would be teaching from," Bill says.

"The lessons Bill presented were solid, biblical messages that tapped into peoples' *thinking* sides," says Nancy. "We sought to partner with him to tap into peoples' *feeling* side. The drama sketches were designed to impact kids' emotions, to help them identify or resonate with whatever the topic of the day was, and to prepare them to hear the message."

"When it came time for my part in the service and I opened my Bible to teach," says Bill, "the kids were hungry to hear what God in His Word had to say."

In the years to come, the arts continued to be a catalyst for God's work in the hearts of students and adults alike during Willow Creek services.

"I was an atheist and my wife a new Christ follower when I began attending Willow Creek with her around 1979," says Lee Strobel, award-winning author and formerly a journalist for the *Chicago Tribune*. "While my left brain needed to wrestle with the intellectual aspects of faith, God used the arts in Willow's services to help my right brain engage. The drama and music had a way of sneaking up on me and opening me up, so that I would be receptive to the truths of Scripture that my right brain was hearing. In time, my intellect became thoroughly convinced that Christianity is true, and my heart was softened so I could say yes to Jesus Christ."

As Lee continued to grow in his faith, he joined the staff at Willow and eventually served as a teaching pastor. (Lee's bestselling book, *The Case for Christ*, chronicles his journey to faith.)

Today, Willow Creek continues to utilize artists and the arts—music, video, drama, dance—to touch people at a deep emotional level. In addition to its weekend services, Willow Creek's holiday services and special events offer a wide-open "front door" for visitors new to church or just beginning the process of spiritual exploration. For many people, it's the prominent use of the arts in these settings that first opens their hearts and minds to God.

"There is something seamless and powerful about a weekend service or special event that impacts the *whole* person," says Nancy. "It sets the stage for God to do His best work in their lives."

Drama sketches during weekend services help set the tone for the teacher's message. Willow Creek productions such as *Jairus* and Willow's Christmas and Easter services provide ideal opportunities for people to invite their friends. Following these services, friends gather around restaurant tables or in living rooms, where the messages presented prompt natural conversation about spiritual matters.

Music that Rocks the House

Throughout Willow Creek's history, contemporary Christian music has been an integral part of its church services. "In the early years of Willow, the congregation sang only one or two pivotal songs at each weekend service," says Matt Lundgren, Willow's executive director of Programming and Production, "because in the 70s and 80s, most people exploring Christianity were not accustomed to singing in public, and Willow's leadership was committed to eliminating unnecessary barriers that might make people feel so uncomfortable in church that they couldn't tune in to the message. All-out worship happened during Willow Creek's midweek service, New Community, which was strategically designed for believers.

"Today, sociological changes in our culture and a better understanding of what helps believers develop spiritually have led to a shift in the structure and style of our services—another example of methods changing, while the mission remains the same," says Matt. "Willow Creek is as committed as ever to reaching those far from God with the message of Jesus Christ, but today's spiritual explorers are different from those of earlier decades. They are perfectly comfortable talking about spiritual issues. They come through Willow's doors looking to understand what the church is all about. They don't want to be mere spectators. They don't shy away from parts of the service that used to make visitors uncomfortable. They want to be participants, and our weekend programming reflects those sociological shifts. Today, we are 'a singing church,' with a healthy portion of every service dedicated to corporate worship. Weekend messages, once targeted more toward spiritual explorers with something for believers as well, now target both the explorer and the believer *together*. A weekend service for both explorers and believers, coupled with individualized growth opportunities throughout each week, is a strategy that best helps us accomplish our mission in today's culture."

A Message that Matters

Perhaps the most life-changing component of those early church services— and of Willow's weekend services today—is the bridge they help build between theology and real life.

"When we first started out," says Bill, "we knew we must do more than just provide people with theological concepts. God's word is rich with practical advice for everyday living. And the infusion of Scripture into our daily lives is vital to helping each of us grow toward Christ-centeredness. We set out to craft messages that would make a tangible difference in how people live, offering truths straight from the Bible and applying the principles of Christ-centered living to the very real issues people face in their classrooms, living rooms, offices, and hearts.

"Over the years, we've been tremendously blessed by the outstanding line-up of teachers who have taken the stage at Willow—men and women committed to presenting God's Word in a way their listeners can understand," says Bill. As a teaching team today, we continue to 'go for the jugular' when it comes to partnering the hard-hitting truths of Scripture with application that challenges people to live out the no-holds-barred call of God on their lives."

The Thirty-Minute Footprint
The early church in Acts 2 experienced exponential growth. Occasionally, large crowds came to faith in Jesus Christ following a message from Peter or Paul, but more often the early church grew one person at a time, through outsiders being struck by the noticeable difference in how individual believers lived their lives in community and loved one another. Similarly, God's kingdom at Willow has expanded one person at a time, through friends inviting friends to experience the love of God they find within this body of believers—both in the context of personal relationships and through attendance at Willow services.

A key ingredient in making it possible for friends to invite friends to Willow Creek has been the concept of honoring the thirty-minute "footprint."

By the late 90s, the footprint of people attending Willow Creek extended more than an hour's drive in all directions from its South Barrington campus. People living that far away found it increasingly difficult to bring their friends to visit the church, when it meant an hour or more in the car, each way. It was also growing more and more difficult for Willow families to utilize the weekday ministries for their children, and attend the adult classes, groups, and serving opportunities provided for them, when they had to drive so far. This dilemma gave rise to a significant change at Willow.

One Church, Multiple Locations
"Those who call Willow 'home' were as motivated as ever for their friends to experience God's love and hear the message of Jesus Christ, not only in

High-quality, contemporary-style music is a cornerstone for Willow Creek's weekend services, from the early days to today. Willow Creek's worship teams use music to usher the congregation into God's presence.

the personal setting of an ongoing relationship, but also in the context of the larger church community," Bill says. "But the challenge of distance was making it increasingly hard to do that. So we set out to honor a '30-minute footprint' by launching regional campuses, making it possible for anyone living in Chicagoland to drive no more than 30 minutes to get to a Willow Creek campus."

Today Willow Creek has four regional campuses—in DuPage County, McHenry County, the North Shore, and downtown Chicago—with plans for more regional sites on the horizon. Each Willow Creek campus employs its own campus pastor and staff, and offers many of the same key ministries as the central campus. All campuses enjoy the same great teaching, videocast to the regional sites from the central campus in South Barrington. The regional model has made it easy once again for friends to invite friends to church, and for families to engage more fully in weekday ministries.

Embracing Our Spanish-Speaking Neighbors

Another key Willow Creek expansion, prompted in part by the 30-minute footprint challenge, was the birth of Casa de Luz ("House of Light"), Willow Creek's Spanish-speaking community. More than 115,000 Spanish-speaking residents live within a 30-minute drive of the main campus in South Barrington. In 2005, Willow Creek launched Casa de Luz to bring the message of Christ to this vital community. Mexican musician and pastor Hector Hermosillo agreed to take the helm as pastor of Casa de Luz in 2006. Today Casa is a thriving community of more than 700 believers that augments the spiritual and cultural richness of Willow Creek South Barrington.

"The Casa community is a gift to Willow," says Bill. "making us a stronger, more kingdom-representative community of Christ followers."

TODAY AND BEYOND

Today, thousands of people throughout the Chicago area worship at a Willow Creek campus.

"While we thank God for the growing numbers of people God has brought our way, numbers have never been the goal," says Bill. "It's never been about reaching *the masses*. It's always been—and I hope it will always be—about reaching *one* person, *one* co-worker or neighbor or friend at a time with the life-changing message of Jesus Christ. Then it's about *that one person* experiencing an internal transformation that leads them to be more kind or courageous or compassionate or hopeful. It's about that one person enjoying renewal and restoration in their personal relationships. It's about that one person becoming a part of a larger community of believers that feels like family. It's about that one person becoming an agent of positive change in God's kingdom at home, in their neighborhood, their city, and around the world. *That's* what Willow Creek is about."

ONE CHURCH

MULTIPLE LOCATIONS

"Willow Creek is not a very traditional church," says Bill, "but one tradition has become very dear to us: We end every Christmas service by singing 'Silent Night.' During the singing of those verses, people are invited to express words of love to the family or friends who came with them. For those moments, I have the best view in the house. I never tire of seeing people embracing, perhaps grieving together the loved one no longer with them and speaking words of love to one another. It's a powerful experience, and one we've grown to treasure as a church family."

03 FULLY DEVOTED

03
FULLY DEVOTED
DISCIPLESHIP

"Prior to coming to Willow Creek, I had 'church' in my life," says Brad,[18] "but once I started attending Willow Creek, I began to have *God* in my life—and there is a *big* difference. I learned that God has been there for me all along, even in the tough years when I couldn't recognize Him. Because of the teachings at Willow Creek, I am learning how to hear Him, talk to Him, and recognize His grace."

otooo

"Thank you, Willow Creek, for making us uncomfortable with how we are going through life," says Barbara.[19] "Thanks for challenging us so we can live the way God intends us to live. Thanks to Bill [Hybels] for not letting up on the importance of relational reconciliation. God has helped me reconcile my broken relationship of 16 years with my family. I was able to see my Dad for the first time in 15 years, just four hours before he died. God was with me that day and I have felt His peace every day since."

otooo

"All my life, I thought I was a Christian," says Pat.[20] "But it wasn't until I was invited to Willow Creek by my own teenage children, who were attending Son City, that I learned about God's grace and what it means to have a personal relationship with Jesus Christ. God was very gentle but persistent as He slowly revealed these concepts to me through the teaching at Willow. I started coming to New Community on Wednesday evenings and eventually accepted Jesus as my Lord and Savior. He then led me through the steps I needed to grow as a believer—including serving and joining a small group. Today, my husband, my children and their spouses, and all my grandchildren are Christ followers. Thank you Jesus and Willow Creek for helping me grow toward being a fully devoted follower of Jesus Christ."

otooo

Lisa[21] states, "We were drawn to visit Willow Creek for the first time three summers ago. Friends who had attended Willow for years showed us around, and helped us get connected. Today, my family is flourishing in Christ! We are growing spiritually together and are genuinely interested in the things of God. We love going to church together, and allowing Christ to teach us how to live out our faith. My husband sits on the edge of his seat, learning from the weekend teachers. My boys experienced God in a powerful and deep way at Sandblast [Willow Creek's high school summer camp], and our Sunday rides to church show the growth God is doing in our family. That's Jesus at work in our lives, through His body at Willow! In my journal, yesterday, I was compelled to list as many things as possible that I thank the Lord for; Willow is near the top of the list. Thank You, Lord, for Willow!"

otooo

For Linda,[22] her journey with Willow paralleled her journey toward sobriety. "I got baptized at Willow in the summer of 2002, even though I was not yet a recovering alcoholic—I was still trying to control my drinking," she says. "But I was slowly being drawn back to God. When I finally got sober in 2005, I began attending both the South Barrington and the Chicago campuses. Since then, I have taken various Willow Creek classes, joined a Blitz

Build project in the Austin area of Chicago, and sing regularly with the 'All God's People Choir' at the Chicago campus. I sense perhaps my next step will be to lead a small group of recovering alcoholics who might be exploring whether Jesus is their Higher Power. I have a long way to go in terms of biblical knowledge, but my Willow classes, as well as weekend services, have benefitted me so much already!"

otooo

"In 1981, my cousin encouraged me to try the singles group at Willow Creek," says Lee.[23] "I knew Christ, but really needed to be connected with other Christians. God used the people in the Prime Time singles ministry to cheer me on toward genuine love and good deeds. The first small group I joined studied the life of King David. From that study, I began to see how these ancient stories in God's Word could have a practical impact on my life and character."

otooo

"My husband and I were at the end of our ropes in our marriage," says Debbie,[24] "and our search for godly solutions led us to Willow Creek. The first message we heard was John Ortberg's launch of the series, 'Storms of Life.' We felt like he was talking just to us. We were so touched by God that we came again on Wednesday and then back on Saturday. Three years later, we became participating members, but it took only that first night for us to totally surrender all we were to Christ—all we thought, all we did, and all we had. The journey since has been an amazing adventure we would not have missed for anything! We love our church and we love our pastor. We are in for life on the journey we are making together."

otooo

"I am in no way the same man I was the first day I walked through the doors of Willow 23 years ago," says Anthony.[25] "I've served with great people, I've been mentored, and now I mentor other men in the CARS Ministry. My wife and I have gone through Divorce Recovery, Marriage Matters, the budget ministry, and we have both gladly served in a variety of ways out of gratitude for how God brought together two broken people and made us one through the help of the church. We are forever grateful to God, the teachers, and three mentors[26] from Willow who have helped us have a strong, godly marriage."

otooo

Kym's[27] spiritual journey has been forever marked by God's hand in her life: "In the 20-plus years I've been a part of Willow, many messages from the weekend services have affected how I live my everyday life. Challenges to read the Bible daily, and listen to and obey God's promptings are just a few ways the teachings at Willow have changed me. I've learned to be a better parent and wife, and I've learned to serve. As a result of serving as a leader in Willow's Prison Ministry, I have become far more compassionate. I've learned, 'You will not find a greater peace than when you're serving the Lord by serving others.' God is amazing!"

otooo

"When I first came to Willow, I believed in God," Bruce[28] says, "but my life was shattered in a million pieces. I knew I couldn't put myself back together again. Back then, I was a broken participant in Divorce Recovery; now, I'm a newly married table leader for this amazing ministry. Then, I couldn't find direction in my own life, but for the past five years, I have served on the traffic team where I *literally* help others find direction! Today, I am on a life-long path of becoming a fully devoted follower. This is a life I could not have created for myself. God took the million pieces of my life and made a new man of me."

otooo

"They devoted themselves to the apostles' teaching and to the fellowship, to the breaking of bread and to prayer. Everyone was filled with awe, and many wonders and miraculous signs were done by the apostles. —Acts 2:42–43

"From this snapshot of everyday life in the early church," says Bill Hybels, "we see that the first century followers of Jesus were fully devoted to Him and to one another. Just a short time earlier, many of these believers had witnessed Jesus' ascension to heaven, and clearly they took His final words seriously." According to the closing verses of Matthew's gospel, Jesus gave His followers these parting instructions:

Then Jesus came to them and said, "All authority in heaven and on earth has been given to me. Therefore go and make disciples of all nations, baptizing them in the name of the Father and of the Son and of the Holy Spirit, and teaching them to obey everything I have commanded you. And surely I am with you always, to the very end of the age." —Matthew 28:18–20

As Jesus handed His followers the mission of joining with God as He establishes His kingdom "on earth as it is in heaven,", He left them with this final challenge: to make *disciples*, people in a redeemed relationship with the Father, Son, and Holy Spirit, who are growing toward Christ-likeness through obedience to Jesus' teachings.

"As we crafted the early priorities and structure of Willow Creek," says Bill, "we took our cue from Jesus' words and challenged ourselves, as well as the new believers at Willow, to become true disciples who were fully devoted to the way of Jesus."

BACK IN THE DAY

Discipleship was the original goal of Bill Hybels' involvement in the 1970s Son City youth group. Bill's friend Dave Holmbo, who started the youth ministry, was a gifted musician so he structured the program around music, creating a large contemporary singing group that rehearsed weekly and performed in local churches. Dave invited Bill to teach a Bible study for these few dozen teens after the weekly rehearsals. Bill utilized the simple format he'd used when leading a college discussion group: he asked the kids to come prepared to focus on a few verses of Scripture, then he'd apply those verses to their everyday life.

Of those first messages, Lynne Hybels recalls, "It soon became evident that Bill had the gift of teaching, though no one was more surprised by that than he.... He was mystified by the impact of his teaching, but those of us who listened weren't. His teaching was practical and relevant, yet thoroughly biblical and challenging and—in an almost uncanny way—empowered."[29]

That format—focusing on a few key passages of Scripture and then applying them to people's lives—has remained fairly unchanged in Willow Creek teaching since those early days. Because God's Word is the bedrock of growing as a disciple of Jesus, it's the foundation upon which Willow's teachers build each message, followed by practical application and strong challenges to live out these biblical truths in our lives.

Paul's second New Testament letter to Timothy paints a vivid description of the power of Scripture to transform believers into the image of Christ.

"Every part of Scripture is God-breathed and useful one way or another—showing us truth, exposing our rebellion, correcting our mistakes, training us to live God's way. Through the Word we are put together and shaped up for the tasks God has for us."
—2 Timothy 3:16 (MSG)

As Son City students responded to the teaching of Scripture and invited their friends to join them, the Bible study grew.

"As increasing numbers of young people came to faith in Christ, it became obvious that we had to become more intentional about helping these young believers grow toward maturity in their faith," Bill says. "Dave began meeting personally with the musicians and artists, mentoring them in their faith, and I began discipling the student leaders. When the group topped 80 kids, we divided it into teams. We continued to disciple the team leaders, who in turn discipled those within their span of care."

A New Community of Believers

When the lessons learned in Son City were adapted to a ministry for all ages and Willow Creek Community Church was launched, the leaders of the new church knew that nurturing believers in their faith must remain a priority. Both long-time Christians and new Christ followers needed to be challenged and equipped to be ever-growing disciples of Jesus.

"Our newly formed Board of Elders carried the responsibility of the spiritual integrity and vitality of the church, as they still do today," explains Bill. "Within months of launching the first service in the Willow Creek Theatre, the Elders realized that our core believers—who were valiantly giving their all to help this upstart church—desperately needed deeper Bible teaching and corporate worship. In January, 1976, we launched the 'New Community,' a midweek gathering specifically designed for discipling Christ followers toward spiritual maturity." The evening presumed of its audience a basic understanding and acceptance of the Christian faith. The biblical messages were much deeper spiritually, and corporate worship played a major role.

Many long-time Willow members look back to those early New Community years as the beginning of their understanding of what full devotion to Jesus means. It's when they first realized that being a Christian is not a one-time decision to "accept Jesus," but an ongoing, ever-deepening process of spiritual transformation.

It Takes a Team

As the church grew, it expanded to multiple services on the weekends with New Community both on Wednesday and Thursday nights. The teaching load became more than one teacher could handle. In order to uphold the value of robust biblical teaching without overtaxing its sole teacher, the Elders endorsed the concept of team teaching. A team of "teaching pastors"—spiritually mature men and women with the gift of teaching—began sharing the teaching responsibilities. While Bill continued to teach the lion's share of the weekend services, these gifted and passionate teachers began sharing the midweek teaching load. By any account, Willow has been the richer for it.

"I'm sure that each member of our congregation can recall with deep fondness the amazing list of teachers whose love of God's Word and ability to share a challenging and inspiring message helped transform their lives," says Bill. "Don Cousins, Nancy Beach, Lee Strobel, John Ortberg, Nancy Ortberg, Gene Appel, Mike Breaux, Randy Frazee, Darren Whitehead, —and others along the way—all have made deep and lasting contributions to the spiritual growth of Willow Creek's congregation. And thanks to technology, many people enjoy their messages again and again on CD or DVD.[30]

Growing Smaller

While a large-group teaching setting is an effective vehicle for spiritual growth, it is not enough. The early church in Acts 2 models the nitty-gritty process of "doing life together" as a key component of discipleship. As Willow grew in size, it became apparent that doing life together was not practical among large groups of people.

"In order to grow bigger, we needed to grow smaller," says Bill. "So we divided the congregation into groups called 'modules—similar to the teams we had established in Son City." These modules became the forerunners to today's small groups—spiritual communities of about a dozen people, where individuals can know one another on a deep level, do life together, and challenge one another toward Christ-likeness.

"Personal growth does not happen in isolation," says Dr. Gilbert Bilezikian, who has championed the Acts 2 community model since Willow's earliest days. The importance of community in the spiritual health of a church cannot be overstated. From our earliest days, community has been crucial in helping individuals, couples, and whole families grow in their spiritual journeys.

Providing strong biblical teaching with real-life application is a long-standing Willow Creek value. Clockwise: Willow Creek Teaching Pastors Bill Hybels, Gene Appel, Mike Breaux, Darren Whitehead, Nancy Beach, Lee Strobel, John Ortberg, Don Cousins, and Casa de Luz Pastor Hector Hermosillo (center) deliver messages that challenge people toward deeper discipleship in Christ.

Small groups come in all shapes and sizes. Some, like women's groups, men's groups, High Road Riders (Willow Creek's motorcycle ministry), and singles groups, are based on a common interest or affinity. Recovery groups, support groups, and workshop discussion groups gather around a shared experience. But whatever the unifying factor, each small group has one overarching goal in mind: Helping its members become more fully devoted followers of Jesus Christ.

What Does Spiritual Maturity Look Like?

Scripture paints a broad yet specific brushstroke of what it looks like to be a disciple of Jesus Christ. In addition to the character traits and lifestyle Jesus models for His disciples throughout the four Gospel accounts[31] of His ministry here on earth, the New Testament is rich with specific instruction for how to live as a Christ follower.

The apostle Paul, who wrote many of the epistles (letters) in the New Testament—and who had a firsthand encounter with the radical, life-changing love of Christ—inspires the Christians in Corinth to measure themselves against a vivid description of God's unconditional love—the kind of love Christ followers (and many a bride and groom) are encouraged to show to one another.

Love is patient, love is kind. It does not envy, it does not boast, it is not proud. It is not rude, it is not self-seeking, it is not easily angered, it keeps no record of wrongs. Love does not delight in evil but rejoices with the truth. It always protects, always trusts, always hopes, always perseveres. Love never fails.
                                                                —1 Corinthians 13:4–8

Paul begins with love when he challenges the disciples from Galatia to desire "fruit of the Spirit"—traits that reflect the type of character Jesus demonstrated throughout His life on earth. Then he identifies specific behaviors consistent with being a truly loving, Christ-like person.

But the fruit of the Spirit is love, joy, peace, patience, kindness, goodness, faithfulness, gentleness and self-control. Against such things there is no law.
                                                                —Galatians 5:22–23

John, arguably Jesus' closest friend, dedicates an entire letter (the book of 1 John) to spelling out what it looks like to love as Jesus loves. His words include:

Dear friends, let us love one another, for love comes from God. Everyone who loves has been born of God and knows God. Whoever does not love does not know God, because God is love. This is how God showed his love among us: He sent his one and only Son into the world that we might live through him. This is love: not that we loved God, but that he loved us and sent his Son as an atoning sacrifice for our sins. Dear friends, since God so loved us, we also ought to love one another. No one has ever seen God; but if we love one another, God lives in us and his love is made complete in us. —1 John 4:7–12

Such worthy, though challenging, goals highlight the importance of disciple-ship as a never-ending process of transformation.

A Little Self-Examination...

"I've been a Christ follower since I was 17 years old," says Bill. "And I still make it a regular habit to do a self-evaluation, to check my life against the values I find in Scripture. How do I measure up today? Where do I need to be growing?"

One method of self-evaluation used at Willow for many years is based on five key components that tend to characterize those growing as disciples of Jesus. They are:

Grace: Have I truly accepted God's forgiveness of sin based solely on the redemptive act of Jesus' death on the Cross and Resurrection?

Growth: Am I practicing spiritual disciplines such as prayer, Scripture reading, corporate worship, and community that will help me grow toward Christ-likeness?

Group: Am I part of a community of Christ followers who do life together, encouraging and challenging one another to live out the call of Jesus on their lives.

Gifts: Am I offering our unique, God-given talents, spiritual gifts, and time for the purpose of furthering God's kingdom here on earth?

Good Stewardship: Am I being responsible caretakers of all God has given, including my time, possessions, resources, and finances?

"As we examine our own lives in light of the values expressed in Scripture and from God," says Bill, "we may discover areas of our lives where He needs to do some pruning and we need to do some growing. The trick is knowing *how* to grow in this direction. What, specifically, do we need to *do* to make progress in that particular area?"

Thankfully, over the years, Willow has offered countless opportunities for people to take "next steps" spiritually. From classes to one-on-one mentoring relationships, from prayer circles to accountability groups, God has used myriad vehicles to help foster spiritual growth. Today it is no different. In fact, in recent years Willow leaders have learned a lot about what it takes to help people grow spiritually through a project called Reveal.

Reveal: How Do People Grow?

"Starting in 1992, we began offering anonymous surveys every three years or so, to our Willow Creek congregation to help us understand things like who was coming to our church, where they lived, and how old they were," says Greg Hawkins, Willow Creek's Executive Pastor. "Those results provided surprising insights, some of which resulted in the regional campuses mentioned earlier.

When we began preparing for our 2003 survey, we worked with a management consultant to help us craft a different kind of survey—one that would help us understand what was going on *inside* of people. What were their spiritual beliefs and attitudes? What were their church and personal activities? This was the beginning of the Reveal survey. It helped us begin to understand how people actually do grow spiritually, and what role the local church can play to help catalyze an individual's movement toward deeper intimacy with Christ.

"In 2007, we extended this work to include other churches to see what we could learn about triggers for spiritual growth. Were there common themes? Common struggles? Common turning points? What could we learn, empirically, about the key components that enhance spiritual growth, not just within Willow's walls but among believers all across the country.

"Today, more than 280,000 congregants in more than 1,200 churches of all shapes and sizes have participated in the Reveal survey," Greg says. "This broad database has provided dramatic insights into what helps people grow in their love of God and others. Reveal has become more than a survey. It has become a discipleship framework around which we can most effectively help one another grow toward Christ-centeredness."

Increased understanding about how to move people toward Christ-centeredness allows churches to direct ministries, staff, and volunteer initiatives toward that end. The statistical data gathered through Reveal, when filtered through the Holy Spirit's guidance, has allowed Willow leaders to become better stewards of our people and resources.

"As a result of Reveal, we have learned that people in today's society grow in a highly individualized way within the community setting," says Greg. "This better understanding has led to a more effective strategy of providing multiple, individualized learning opportunities throughout the week, rather than the 'one-size-fits-all' approach of a single midweek service that had worked so well for many years."

Midweek and weekend classes offer individualized learning opportunities to help people make forward progress in their spiritual journey.

As a result of the findings in the Reveal survey, Willow Creek better understands how people move toward spiritual maturity in Christ. Below: Bill Hybels draws the Reveal Spiritual Continuum to show how people grow from Exploring Christ (Exp) to Beginning Christian (Beg) to Close to Christ (C), toward Christ-Centered (CC).

"Another result of our findings through Reveal," adds Bill, "is the affirmation that **regular Bible reading is vital to spiritual growth**. This has always been a key value, not only of Willow as a whole, but in my personal life. I find it necessary for my own spiritual growth to have a ruthless commitment to early morning times of solitude, when I can study a passage of Scripture, then spend extended time in prayer, confession, journaling, and quietly listening for God's voice. Today's culture makes it challenging to carve out daily, uninterrupted time. But it is absolutely essential for me. *Nothing* gets me to budge off that early morning practice that keeps me rooted and grounded and quiet and sane."

This kind of dogged commitment to Scripture reading and the regular practice of spiritual disciplines is the key ingredient for anyone who takes their own spiritual growth seriously. God's Word, when it penetrates the human heart, will not fail to produce fruit in the form of a life transformed in the image of Christ. While not everyone is an early morning person, every Christ follower seeking to grow, needs to find *and ruthlessly protect* some regular, consistent time for personal Bible study and prayer.

"In the end, my spiritual growth and discipleship is no one's responsibility but my own," Bill says. "It's not the church's job, it's not my small group's job, it's not my spouse's job. Part of becoming a fully devoted follower of Christ is learning to be a self-feeder, pulling ourselves up to the table of spiritual disciplines, grabbing our own fork, and feeding ourselves with the vital practices and habits that will result in growth.

"Willow is blessed with a staff committed to building ministries, classes, workshops, and myriad other growth-producing opportunities," Bill continues. "But at the end of the day, it's not the church's job to grow us. It's yours. It's mine. Each of us bears full responsibility for engaging in the spiritual disciplines necessary to move toward Christ-likeness. That's a huge responsibility, but it pays big dividends, bearing bountiful fruit in our lives."

Student Impact leader Kristin Hogan and high school girls Jennifer Wink, Jessica Wink, and Karie Butler have been doing life together as a small group since 2006. (Not pictured: Sarah Bach and Becky Segriff)

04
FULLY UNITED
COMMUNITY

"He'd just as soon punch you in the nose as say hello," says Mike's mother, Karen.[32] At 21, he was a hardened kid; his drinking had landed him in the hospital and then rehab. But one Saturday night, after listening over and over again to a cassette tape of a Bill Hybels' message on compassion, Mike attended a Willow Creek service.

"I'd grown up with enough religious ritual to last me a lifetime," says Mike,[33] "so I wanted nothing to do with church. But for me, that night was the turning point. I'd never felt the sense of community that was so apparent here.

Authentic, biblical relationships are the bedrock of Axis, Willow Creek's 18 to 20-something community.

Not long after, I gave my life to Christ. My support group saw me through my darkest days. They walked with me toward a changed life."

Mike introduced his mom to Willow, who in turn brought her other children and her husband, Phil. They have all come to Christ here, along with grand-children and countless friends and neighbors. Today, Mike is happily married with two children, and is celebrating 18 years of sobriety. Every Christmas, he partners with a local rehab center to bring a busload of kids to Willow and introduce them to God. "I remember all too well what it felt like to be where they are at," Mike says. "And I just want them to find the hope and healing I found here through my Willow community."

otooo

"I came to Willow Creek North Shore (WCNS) after my husband of 30 years divorced me," says Aiko.[34] "WCNS is a safe environment where I can hear God's Word and experience His grace. I have been able to express my need for Him, let go of my perfectionism, and begin to trust others. I've found a place where my feelings and opinions are valued. I thank my God for the incredible Christ-centered community at Willow Creek and for my North Shore family."

otooo

"After two years of marriage," Theresa[35] says, "I discovered my Christian hus-band was a sex addict and had been cheating on me the whole time. Soon after, we found Faithful & True [Willow's recovery groups for sexual broken-ness]. This community provided us with acceptance, hope, support, safety, encouragement, and God's healing. We've been in recovery for eight years now. We just celebrated our 10th anniversary and gave birth to our second child. Without God providing Willow's recovery ministries, I would have left my husband eight years ago and missed out on all of God's blessings—including our two beautiful children. Rest assured, God is using Willow!"

otooo

"Granted, Willow Creek is a large church, but to me it has truly been like the little neighborhood church on the corner," says Catherine.[36] "Community is one of the cornerstones of Willow Creek, and as a single, fully devoted Christ follower, Willow has provided me with community through different small groups and ministries over the years. I believe we enjoy the same warm, spirit-fed community today as those who were a part of the Acts 2 church did two thousand years ago. Thank you, Willow Creek!"

otooo

"In 2004, I was living life in a fog," says Donna.[37] "I was going through a divorce and suffering financial loss. God brought healing and friendships into my life through my support group in Divorce Recovery. We supported each other through our divorces, laughed together, cried together, were vulnerable with each other, and have shared many events and get-togethers. Today, we continue to share prayer requests, celebrate birthdays, and encourage each other. I used to be disconnected from others, but now I'm deeply connected in community! I'm no longer lonely, depressed, or hopeless. Willow is the 'anchor' in my life—the place that holds me connected to a strong relationship with the Lord. My friends are my 'oxygen.' They make it easier for me to breathe and cope with life. Today, I'm on the *other* side of despair: I'm a single mom of two teenage girls and now have the privilege of helping other single moms navigate their way through what I have experienced. Yay God for Willow! It's given me community."

otooo

"Our journey to Willow Creek Chicago is a true story of community," says Francis Wyatt, (worship pastor at Willow Creek Chicago's campus). "God put many people in our paths whose generosity and faithfulness paved the way for us to follow God's call and move our family from Ohio to Chicago. We lost money when we sold our Ohio house, and found ourselves with little money and moving to a brand new city we knew nothing about. A wonderful man from Willow Chicago opened his condo to us and our four kids. He even took in our cat! It is humbling to be on the receiving end of financial help—to be the ones 'who had need,' talked about in Acts 2. But through the community of God's people, we got back on our feet. Financial gifts, practical gifts like reliable transportation and appliances, and even an extra gift—a vacation—are just some of the ways God has provided for us through community. Today, we own our own home, and we have been able to help others like God helped us. All we have, we owe to God!"

otooo

"I had been sexually assaulted," says Kathryn,[38] "and I was filled with shame and despair. One night, I decided to go to a Willow Creek service. When I arrived, I received the warmest, most sincere greeting from one of the Guest Ministry hosts. She didn't know what had happened to me; she didn't know me at all. But in that moment, I felt God's love for me, and I knew I needed a community of God's people in my life. I soon gave my life to Christ, and He has helped me become a better person and get where I am today. I will always remember that night: a warm greeting from a stranger was the turning point in my life because it helped me get on my journey to Christ. Thank you, Guest Ministry! Keep reaching thousands through your loving spirits and hearts."

otooo

Steve[39] found community through a group in his Grayslake neighborhood. "I came into the group five years ago, not knowing what to expect. What I found is an amazing group of people who love God and love one another. Today we have six families in our group, with kids of all ages. We always make sure the kids are included. In addition to our multi-generational group, the men have developed strong relationships and meet for Bible study, and the women meet together as well. We even go on an annual Wisconsin retreat together. I'm blessed to be part of a great church that led me to a group of God-loving people, right here in Grayslake!"

otooo

"When I moved to Chicago many years ago," says Tara,[40] "I was searching for a new church home and a chance to start over. I began attending the Axis service at Willow, where I found hundreds of 20-somethings committed to following Christ. I was intrigued, yet nervous. I had not allowed God or people close to me in many years. Would this community of believers accept me for who I truly am—my present as well as my past? As I began to share my life story, these people gave me loving encouragement, acceptance, and challenging truths. I rededicated my life to Christ, and felt the weight of years of regret fall from my shoulders. Meeting God and His community at Willow has changed my life's trajectory—and for that, I will be forever grateful."

otooo

"I was fortunate to find the HighRoad Riders [Willow's motorcycle ministry] and their small group in 2009, when I was going through a divorce," says Vicki.[41] "I experienced Christian community firsthand when these motorcycle-riding Christ followers allowed me to share the pain I was going through and made me feel welcome. They are definitely a community of believers doing God's work. Thank you, HighRoad Riders and Willow Creek. God used you to make a huge positive impact on my life."

otooo

Robbie and Gary[42] have being doing life with a community of friends at Willow since 1990. "When we first came to Willow," Robbie says, "my husband feared we'd never feel at home or find our place. But he participated in a Camp Paradise work week and built strong friendships with some of the men there. It was the beginning of his ministry passion and the start of our deep friendships with amazing people. Throughout the years we've laughed, cried, eaten, worshipped, celebrated, grieved, and prayed with each other.

When my husband was diagnosed with cancer, this community of friends was there, visiting us, bringing food, running errands, driving to chemo, painting our house, and even purchasing major medical equipment. My husband was promoted to heaven on June 18, 2009—the opening day of the Camp Paradise season. Coincidence? I think not. Camp Paradise friends are our angels of mercy—a true community of believers."

Every day they continued to meet together in the temple courts. They broke bread in their homes and ate together with glad and sincere hearts, praising God and enjoying the favor of all the people. —Acts 2:46–47a

Doing life together—spending time in one another's homes, sharing meals, experiencing sincere relationships, finding practical support, growing closer to God, and welcoming newcomers into the intimate community they enjoyed— was the norm for the early church. And it's no wonder. They spent three years following a Rabbi who lived out community to its fullest.

Jesus and His band of twelve disciples traveled the countryside, village to village, as He proclaimed the kingdom of God. They shared meals, witnessed miracles, listened to temple teachings, received correction, were challenged toward growth, and experienced a relational connection beyond their wildest dreams. Jesus had a larger circle of friends—some 70 or so followers who were also part of His group. And He also had a smaller, inner circle: Peter, James, and John. Scripture even indicates Jesus had a "best friend," John, described as "the disciple Jesus loved."[43]

But biblical community—the profound experience of knowing and being known, loving and being loved—pre-dates the early church, and it pre-dates Jesus' earthly ministry. In fact, community goes all the way back to God Himself—the triune God of Christianity, represented in the persons of the

Father, the Son, and the Holy Spirit—in perfect relationship with one another, each fully individual and together fully One. This trinity of God represents community in its perfect form.

We see the "community" language God uses about Himself in the first verses of Scripture:

Then God said, "Let us make human beings in our image, to be like us."
—Genesis 1:26a (NLT)

"People are hard-wired for intimate relationships with one another," says Bill Hybels. "Created in the image of a triune God, every fiber of our being yearns for the relational fulfillment found only through God-centered community."

The bond of community shared by Jesus' disciples and followers showed itself in those agonizing days between Jesus' death on the Cross and the empty tomb of Easter morning. As had been their habit throughout Jesus' ministry, the community of Christ followers turned to one another in their sorrow, confusion, and pain. And in the close-knit confines of the upper room where they met, the Holy Spirit that Jesus had promised came into their midst, infusing each individual with the Spirit of God, and drawing them into a powerful unity that swelled like a tidal wave upon first-century Jerusalem, Judea, and beyond.

"The Holy Spirit shows up and fills these 120 or so believers," says Bill, "and community is catalyzed. More than 3,000 people witness the Holy Spirit's activity in that small gathering of people and come to Christ. This is still the pattern today: when God's people open wide the door of their hearts to Him, they are forever changed, and they are drawn into the kind of Spirit-infused relationships that characterized the early church. Community like that is contagious. Authentic, God-infused, Holy Spirit-ignited community draws people to Christ."

BACK IN THE DAY

The little group of high school students, who made up the original Son City crowd, experienced this kind of God-infused community. As Scripture came alive to these teens through anointed teaching and their lives were transformed through the disciplines of personal study and prayer, something supernatural clicked in.

"The fire of the Holy Spirit absolutely ignited these kids," Lynne Hybels recalls. "They responded immediately and radically to whatever they learned. If Bill taught on relational reconciliation, as soon as the meeting was over students searched for people they had a problem with and began a reconciliation process. They were equally committed to sharing their resources. Kids fortunate enough to have cars drove miles out of their way to pick up others who needed a ride. If a group of kids went out for coffee after a meeting, whoever happened to have money that week paid for those who didn't. Kids with trouble at home were welcomed into the homes of other students—for as long as necessary. When someone asked for prayer, students gathered in groups immediately to ask for God's intervention. Every contribution a student made—from teaching a Bible study to baking cupcakes to playing the drums to cleaning up after an event—no matter how great or small—was appreciated and esteemed by their peers. Students marginalized at school because of physical or mental disabilities were given extra attention and honor at Son City. And it wasn't just isolated groups of students who entered into this kind of community; everybody was busy giving and receiving love, busy serving and being served."

Son City's compelling teaching and programming undoubtedly attracted many first-time visitors, but what kept them coming back was the raw, authentic, love-soaked community they discovered. At Son City, students were stunned by the sheer power of being loved beyond measure by the God of the universe—and by their peers.

This is community—people experiencing God's love firsthand. It's a place to know and be known, to give and receive love, to serve, to laugh, to cry, to belong, to do life as part of a greater whole. Throughout Willow Creek's existence, biblical community has been the foundation upon which the life of the church is built. It was steeped into the very DNA of Son City, and it's an essential part of Willow's genetic makeup today.

THROUGH THE YEARS

"For 35 years, we watched the community that had developed between Son City students 'grow up' and remake itself in the context of moms and dads, brothers and sisters, singles and seniors," says Bill. "During those years we looked for rules or principles we could apply to the development of biblical community. Was there a relational system we could structure that would guarantee community? Or would true biblical community only flow from a series of connections that developed organically? Or as it completely dependent upon us teaching the correct relational principles? We discovered that yes, correct teaching is important. Relational principles about love, reconciliation, encouragement, honesty, and others—if taught regularly—will foster the natural growth of community. But beyond this, rules don't seem to apply. Biblical community can be found *anywhere* Christ followers gather:"

On an early morning each week, six retired men gather around the fireplace in Dr. B's Café, steaming coffees and Bible study materials in hand. After giving their answers to the prepared study questions, their conversation naturally expands to embrace stories of celebration or heartache, stories that patiently waited their turn behind the study questions. An "official" Willow small group with a recommended curriculum provides a pathway to matters of the heart. *This is community.*

On any Thursday evening, you can find a half dozen 20-somethings sitting around a table in a dark sports bar, eating pizza and talking about their lives. They don't do a Bible study or work through prepared curriculum, but it's not uncommon for them to encourage or challenge each other with a Scripture passage. And if anyone around that table is carrying a burden, they won't be carrying it alone when they leave. *This too is community.*

Willow staff will continue to provide a wide range of options for people to gather in structured groups formed around a common stage of life, common challenge, or common interest, knowing that such groups often provide a setting where authentic community grows. As a church, Willow will also continue to recognize that often true biblical community develops organically, with no formal connection to any church program or structure. What has become clear during the past 35 years is that community happens when individuals—transformed by the Holy Spirit—say yes to following Jesus on the pathway of giving and receiving, growing, loving, and serving—all in the context of intimate, mutual relationships. And anyone who follows Him down this path, experiences a little foretaste of heaven.

TODAY AND BEYOND

Our world is aching for community—for the connection to God and one another that has been built into the human heart since the dawn of time. Those without Christ sense the community void in their souls. In its frenetic search to fill this void, today's culture is looking for the quick fix. Increasingly, face-to-face human interaction is replaced with screen-to-screen connections through social media. Addictions to drugs, alcohol, and gambling are at an all-time high, and because of the near-effortless accessibility to internet porn, sociologists are predicting a tidal wave of addiction to pornography and fractured relationships in the coming generation. For lack of the deep, relational connections for which we were created, we anesthetize ourselves with devastating, dime-store substitutions. So where is the hope?

"The hope of this generation and the next lies in Christ-centered community," Bill says. "There is no substitute, no short cut for true Christian community to fill the void in our souls. The safety of kitchen-table conversations, the comfort of people who show up at the hospital when tragedy strikes, the growth-producing effect of friends willing to hold a mirror up to your life so you can see the smudges as well as the beauty—these form the very fabric of community known as the church. And there is nothing more beautiful to behold."

Community Comes in All Shapes and Sizes

Promiseland: Offered during all weekend services, Promiseland seeks to help children develop an authentic, age-appropriate faith in Jesus Christ that will mature throughout their lives. Kids experience biblical community and grow in their relationship with God through discussion, learning activities, and prayer. "We believe the most influential community in a child's life is in their home," says Pat Cimo, Willow's Promiseland and Family Life director. "Kids who see their parents living out an authentic faith are most likely themselves to develop a faith that sticks. By providing parenting resources, workshops, and social events, Promiseland partners with parents to help them fulfill their role as their child's spiritual leader."

Elevate: In Elevate, Willow's junior high ministry, students and leaders join together in a community characterized by challenge, support, and personal growth. "In the three years we have a student in our ministry, we do our best to teach them skills that will help them become and remain followers of God," says Elevate director Scott Rubin. "Hopefully, what they learn in Elevate will help them navigate junior high—and will stick with them throughout the rest of their lives."

Student Impact: Student Impact, Willow Creek's high school ministry, helps students grow spiritually through Sunday worship gatherings, house groups (small groups meeting in local neighborhoods), and The Uprising—student-led campus groups at area high schools. "We're building a community of students passionately following Jesus in a way that compels others to follow Him," says Student Impact director Shane Farmer.

Casa de Luz: Biblical community is the heartbeat of Casa de Luz, Willow's Spanish language congregation, where people connect with their Spanish-speaking neighbors through neighborhood events, small groups, and weekend services.

Serving Groups: Friendships and faith are forged in serving groups as people use their talents, gifts, and time to make a difference in God's kingdom by volunteering together in ministries across the church, neighborhood, city, and world.

Camp Paradise: During a spring work camp, grandfathers, fathers, and sons get muddy preparing the rustic Camp Paradise campgrounds for a summer's worth of Father-Son and Father-Daughter camp sessions. Located on the Tahquamenon River in Northern Michigan—and featuring no electricity or running water—generations of dads and kids have forged community together under the stars, where the stillness of the forest makes God's voice a little easier to hear.

Guest Ministry: In a larger church like Willow Creek, creating a warm, inviting atmosphere is vital to helping people know this is a place they can belong. Guest Ministry hosts delight in helping someone new to Willow feel at home.

Prayer Team: Willow Creek's weekend prayer team prays with people before and after services. A weekday prayer team prays for requests submitted online and by phone, bringing each specific request before God.

Singles: Being a single adult is not a circumstance to be solved, but a unique opportunity to grow in faith and serve in community. Willow Creek singles in their 30s, 40s, and 50s meet for small groups, serving opportunities, and monthly gatherings.

Seniors: Willow Creek seniors involved in "60+" build relationships with other active adults, address the practical needs of those in the second half of life, and use their gifts, abilities, and life experiences to make a unique contribution to the ministry of Willow. Monthly meetings, day trips, serving opportunities, small groups, and a vibrant prayer ministry are all designed to help seniors move forward in their spiritual journey within the context of a close-knit community.

Men: Willow Creek Men's Breakfasts, located in neighborhoods throughout Chicagoland, equip men to discover who God made them to be, focus on His role in their lives, and do life together in a small group setting.

Women: Women at Willow Creek pursue full devotion to Jesus Christ in a community context of intimate friendships, Bible studies, and Women's Daytime Classes.

HighRoad Riders: This community of motorcycle enthusiasts develop friendships and grow spiritually by riding together and enjoying time in social settings where they share insights into what it means to be a Christian.

Recovery and Support: We live in a broken world, but we don't have to live there alone. Willow Creek recovery groups, support groups, and workshop discussion groups help people navigate the storms of life by providing a safe place to be heard, encouraged, and supported—a community where they can heal and grow.

Special Friends: Willow Creek's Special Friends ministry is a community of believers committed to reaching out to people with disabilities and their families. At the annual Special Friends Fishing Derby, individuals with disabilities, their families, friends, and caregivers enjoy a carnival-like atmosphere with great food, and—hopefully—the thrill of landing a fish!

Harvest Food Court and Dr B's Café: Great food and beverages help create an atmosphere that nourishes community, a place where friends can meet and share their lives with one another over a meal or a cup of Fair Trade coffee. Profits from both Harvest and Dr. B's are directed to support Willow Creek's compassion initiatives.

DadFest: For the dad, brother, or neighbor who might otherwise think church has nothing to interest them, a church invitation is easy to extend every Father's Day weekend, when Willow Creek's CARS Ministry hosts DadFest—a car show, live music, kid's activities, and free hot dogs that create a contagious atmosphere of community in Willow Creek's parking lot.

Life change happens best in community. "Our men's group has been meeting together for many years," says Otis Price (far right), Willow Creek Elder. "We've stuck together through thick and thin. We've raised our kids together. Relationships like these last a lifetime."

05 FULLY INVESTED

Global Leadership Summit, Beijing, China
"I love the fact that our pure mission is to help other churches prevail," says Bill Hybels, "to help them meet their God-given calling to model His love in their neighborhoods, their cities, and their countries. We place a serving towel over our arm for the purpose of helping local churches around the world to reach their full redemptive potential."

FULLY INVESTED
ENGAGING THE GLOBAL CHURCH

"I am the kind of guy who finds food and wants others to find the food as well," says Rony.[44] "After attending Willow Creek's conference for church leaders, The Global Leadership Summit (GLS), here in Guatemala, I felt called from the Lord to help train other pastors. My dream is to keep on developing teams who can bring the GLS training to the rural areas of Guatemala, so the pastors and lay leaders there can have encouragement and passion to do the work of the Lord."

ⲟⲧⲟⲟⲟ

Global Leadership Summit, Johannesburg, South Africa
"Whenever we hold a conference in another country," says Bill, "any finances realized in that country stay in-country for the work of the local church there." This differentiates the WCA from almost every other international ministry in the world.

"The principles and creativity our children's ministry team brought home from the very first Willow Creek children's ministry conference transformed our mid-sized neighborhood church in Spokane, Washington," says Sandy.[45] "Our volunteer staff came home more passionate than ever about their vital role in helping children develop an ever-deepening relationship with Jesus. Their commitment to reaching kids and their families for Christ skyrocketed. Within a year or two, our sleepy little Sunday School program had become a can't-miss destination for kids each week, and their parents began to understand the importance of spiritual growth, not only for their children, but in their own lives as well."

otooo

Michael,[46] who attends Willow Creek DuPage, was caught off-guard while serving at The Global Leadership Summit, which first began at Willow Creek South Barrington and now travels to cities across the US and around the globe: "I volunteered for The 2010 Leadership Summit, and was assigned to be Willow's front person at the Summit site in Yuma, Arizona (112 degrees!). As in previous times when I'd volunteered at Willow, I signed up to serve, not because I hoped to receive some benefit, but out of deep gratitude for the total and painful price Jesus paid for me. However, while serving in Yuma and watching the Summit guests laugh, cry, worship, and grow, I was frequently moved to tears with deep joy, appreciation, and thankfulness to God. Without exaggeration, those two days were the richest days of my life. I only played a tiny role in that event, but I realized my role was part of God's redemptive thread stretching across centuries and continents—a process that began 2,000 years ago in Jerusalem and then spread to Asia Minor, Rome, North Africa, Europe, North America, South Barrington—and to Yuma. What a privilege! I was overcome with awe, wonder, and thankfulness. I gave up four days of pay to be in Yuma, but it was well worth it for the wonderful and rich deposits made to my soul. I am proud of God and proud to be a part of His work at Willow."

otooo

"The stories we hear in Africa," says Philip, who lives in Ghana,[47] "are of all the crises in Africa—war, famine, and disease. It is all caused by *egocentric* leadership. My passion is to see [the church in Ghana] raise up *servant* leaders who want to meet the needs of other people. Being part of The Global Leadership Summit is a great joy I want to give to my people. We want their lives to be touched. I believe that if they can listen to even one speaker, one session, it will change their lives. **If you can transform a leader, you can transform a community.** If we can take the GLS from Ghana to Sierra Leone, a country devastated by war, we will change that country. I believe that this is the time, friends, this is the time, and we can take that country for God."

otooo

"Willow Creek Church has impacted my life and church in eternal ways," says Leanne.[48] "I live in Auckland, New Zealand, and in 1998 a business woman who I barely know offered to pay for me to attend The Global Leadership Summit. At the time, I was a young mum and a volunteer at my church. That event opened my eyes to the fact that church didn't have to be the same as it always had been... that it could be real and relevant and make a difference in my life—in fact, it *must* do that, or we were all wasting our time. My husband and I have been to Willow several times since ... and the short story is that our church today has a new culture, and the effects of that are felt far beyond our church community. My husband and I now serve as the lead pastors! Thank you , Willow, for giving us a new vision for an Acts 2 church, for modeling what that looks like, and for equipping us to impact our community in such significant and eternal ways."

otooo

The challenges in Edwin's[49] church seemed insurmountable. "I pastor a church plant that merged with the oldest Baptist church in Brooklyn, New York. We had this church of drug addicts and prostitutes and people with tattoos on their necks merging with this other church of people who had been members for longer than I had been alive. They wore belts that were older than me! Different histories, different backgrounds, different amount of time in Christ. These two groups just didn't have anything in common. But when our leadership team attended the Summit, we found a focused vision. Now, every year at the Summit, we get fed, we get marching orders, we get help, we grow as a leadership team. Our people believe that there is something bigger than we are, something we can do in our corner of the world, that we can bless and influence other people to follow Jesus, to love the Lord, to use the gifts and talents that Jesus has given us for His glory and honor. We dream of one day being as effective and passionate with our gifts as possible, that God will use us to inspire other churches around our community—perhaps some churches that have hit a plateau or are in decline. We dream that one day we will be an influential force in Brooklyn, using what God has given us to glorify Him through our lives."

otooo

"Last year, my wife and two of our good friends joined me in attending The Leadership Summit," says Jim.[50] "We came away inspired! On the drive home, my wife challenged us: 'OK, smart people, what are we going to do with all that we have learned? Surely God can use us!' What followed were some great discussions and several weeks of prayer, research, and listening to God for how the four of us could do something for Him. We came up with several ideas but the one that stuck was Hungerpalooza, a backyard, live music event where we could bring neighborhoods together to raise money for local food banks. Our mission is twofold: 1) To raise money to help feed people who are hungry, and 2) To bring believers and spiritual explorers together in a fun, casual, atmosphere.

"We launched our first Hungerpalooza event, and more than 80 people came. We raised enough money to provide 34,000 meals for our local food bank in DuPage County, Illinois! And the atmosphere was just what we'd hoped; there were all kinds of spiritual conversations going on. God is so good! This summer, we have four Hungerpaloozas planned, with several more in the works.

"I always thought the Leadership Summit was just for church leaders, but it inspires everyone to step up and reach out to others with the love of Christ. God has used the Leadership Summit, our pastors, and all of Willow Creek to truly change my life and my wife's life. They have influenced us to be bold in our pursuit of Christ."

otooo

"The Global Leadership Summit is such a great blessing for my church and in my life," says Oscar.[51] "One of my dreams is to raise up the level of leadership in pastors and leaders in my country, Peru, where godly leadership is the key for anything to get accomplished. Many of them have a lack of studies or experience, and many pastors and leaders must work a regular job during the week and then serve the church on the weekend. Now they are tasting the flavor of the GLS and they are very excited about it."

otooo

Fernando[52] sees The Global Leadership Summit as a key tool God can use to help the Ecuadorian church thrive. "The first Summit I attended, I knew we needed this in my country—in our local church as well as the entire national church—because of the lack of growth and leadership training here. We needed something new, something fresh, something creative, and we found it in the GLS. We are talking about reproducing something similar to take it to people in smaller towns, cities, or different provinces who cannot come to the GLS in the capital city of Quito."

"I grew up in the evangelical church in Egypt," says Fady.[53] "When I came here to the States and attended the GLS, the first thing I thought as I sat in the first session was, 'We have to take this to the Middle East!' Egypt has a very old history, and with this long history come deep cultural issues—poverty, some lack of education, economic challenges. A lot of these challenges in the culture and society tend to show in the local church. Our hopes and dreams for GLS Egypt and for the Arabic-speaking church are to get new generations excited about leading their churches to a new level and to new people. It's an amazing opportunity to introduce Christ-like leadership to all of society. If this generation grasps that, and takes the vision and goes out with the skills they have and the gifts God gives them, I think they will be an amazing light that will shine everywhere."

Julian[54] observes, "In Indonesia, it's not easy if you want to lead a church or become a minister. We are considered the largest Muslim country in the world now, with 240 million people spread across 16,000 islands. We have a lot of different cultures, differences in personality and leadership styles, and the old family culture. Pastors want to know they are not doing this alone. There are people [in churches across the world] who are partnering together with us.

"As an Asian culture, we have learned that there is a challenge between senior leadership and junior leadership. But through these GLS leadership moments, it's a blending of conventional-wisdom leadership with the passionate young leaders. We are praying that all the leadership levels from every area in our nation can join hand in hand, to create a new movement for God in Indonesia."

"The GLS happened in the United Kingdom five years ago," says Graeme.[55] "We have gone from two sites to 18 sites across the nation. The Leadership Summit has teaching that is very adaptable to our culture. The diversity of the teaching, from the secular, to the church, to social justice, meets a need in the nation. Leaders are going away encouraged, inspired, and confident that this is something worth doing. I never stop being amazed by how the Holy Spirit works in the lives of men and women—how they come to these events and their lives are changed; how they go back with a renewed vision to change their management styles in their church and reach more people for Jesus. My dream is that we will continue to grow and reach a needy nation, a nation that once sent missionaries out all across the world. Now it is happening in reverse, and the GLS is answering that need."

otooo

The Democratic Republic of Congo [DRC] in central Africa is considered one of the most corrupt, dangerous places in the world. But its people have hope, and their hope is in Christ-centered leadership. "To bring The Leadership Summit to Congo is to see how God can let leadership transform [people]," says Cedrick,[56] "and to change their lifestyle of corruption, HIV/AIDS, and a kind of discrimination between the top leaders and the low people. The GLS is a way to bring leaders together. It is a challenge because we have poor roads, we have few paved roads, and communication is very difficult. It was very amazing last year, when we did the first GLS in DRC. We expected 800 people, but 1,200 people showed up!

"Leadership is a big issue for the people who lead through the church, through government, businesses, and all sectors in Africa. The dream for GLS in the Congo is to go beyond DRC to all French-speaking countries in Africa. GLS is the new vision for Africa, the new organism to transform Africa."

otooo

The Christian church in Romania has been devastated in recent history. "During the Communist regime," Gelu[57] says, "we lost about 75% of the Romanian evangelical leaders to martyrdom, brutal persecution, being expelled from the country, or being taken to mental institutions. Even today, there is persecution against leaders who would attend [The Global Leadership Summit]. But we really need to provide environments to help the remaining and new Christian leaders develop and make significant contributions to the country. People who attend are looking for hope, and for creative ideas for attacking the issues in their communities such as poverty, injustice, disease, and so on. After we participated in the GLS in Bucharest, we were enthusiastic! The resources are significant in helping change the mindset of the people of Romania and in helping us reach out with the gospel of Jesus Christ."

All the believers were together…   —Acts 2:44a

These five short words—nestled quietly in the middle of a technicolor picture of community—shed light on the counter-cultural phenomenon of the early church.

"In a first-century society where it matters very much who you are, where you are born, whether you are a Pharisee or a shepherd, a Roman citizen or a slave," says Bill Hybels, "these five little words, '*All the believers were together,*' are mind-blowing. They set the stage for a landmark trait of Christian community: oneness. There is no room for 'us' and 'them' in the body of Christ. All believers belong together. No one is left standing on the wayside. No one is excluded from the circle. Followers of Jesus Christ belong to one another. They are *together.*"

Jesus' final recorded prayer, found in the Gospel of John, reveals the potential impact of what can happen when Christ followers come together in unity:

May [My followers] experience such perfect unity that the world will know that You sent Me and that You love them as much as You love Me.
                                                        —John 17:23 (NLT)

The apostle Paul, too, emphasizes this picture of oneness in his letter to the believers in Galatia:

For you are all children of God through faith in Christ Jesus. And all who have been united with Christ in Baptism have put on Christ, like putting on new clothes. There is no longer Jew or Gentile, slave or free, male and female. For you are all one in Christ Jesus.   —Galatians 3:26–28 (NLT)

In the spirit of oneness, the church is to care for all its members. To the Christ followers in Corinth, Paul uses the word picture of our physical bodies to convey the complete connectedness of Jesus' followers.

The body is a unit, though it is made up of many parts; and though all its parts are many, they form one body. So it is with Christ.... Now the body is not made up of one part but of many... so that there should be no division in the body, but that its parts should have equal concern for each other. If one part suffers, every part suffers with it; if one part is honored, every part rejoices with it. Now you are the body of Christ, and each one of you is a part of it.
—1 Corinthians 12:12, 14, 25–27

As the early church grew and spread throughout the ancient Near East, the physical distance between local bodies of believers increased, but the value of oneness remained. Today, the global church spreads to almost every corner of the earth and is represented through countless denominational expressions. And while differences in sacraments, emphases on varying points of theology, and—sadly—some ugly eras in Christian history don't exactly paint a perfect picture of unity, Jesus' call for oneness among His followers remains the call of the global church today.

What does it look like to live out this call? For today's believers, is it "out of sight, out of mind" or is there a way to stay connected despite the barrier of distance? How can a local group of Christ followers exhibit a spirit of oneness with other local churches around the world? For Willow Creek, an opportunity for global oneness presented itself in the mid-1980s.

BACK IN THE DAY

God provided Willow Creek a place to call home—a beautiful piece of land with room to grow. The fire of compassion for friends far from God burned brightly at this new location, as it had in the old Willow Creek Theatre in Palatine, Illinois.

"For reasons only God can explain, Willow Creek was blessed with rapid growth," says Lynne Hybels. "As the power of the Holy Spirit continued to draw more and more people into the circle of community, other churches and the media began to take note. Bill began receiving phone calls from pastors curious to understand what God was doing at Willow. Calls from Dallas, Seattle, and New York soon expanded to calls from Sydney, London, Paris, and Munich. 'What is God up to?' these pastors wondered, 'And how can we get Him to do it in *our* cities, too?'"

"At the time, our leaders and staff were up to their eyeballs in equipping their volunteers and expanding Willow's ministries to meet the needs of our growing congregation," says Bill. "We didn't have the bandwidth to stop and evaluate what God was doing, let alone the wisdom to share some sort of strategy with other pastors. I knew it wasn't some sort of church leadership strategy that was growing Willow—it was the white-hot fire of the Holy Spirit imparting Himself through individuals with hungry hearts and willing hands. Frankly, I wasn't too confident that what was happening at Willow was transferrable. Would the things that seemed to be effective for a middle-class, Midwestern, Willow Creek audience translate to the west coast, New England, or Texas—let alone across national borders and cultures? Could the outpouring of the Holy Spirit here be communicated and encouraged at churches far away?"

But as the requests from far-away pastors escalated, Bill eventually agreed to meet with a group of 26 pastors who were willing to fly in from their various locations and gather for a loosely formatted time of Q & A. "I just had to show up and answer their questions about God's activity at Willow," Bill recalls. "Little did I know what ripple effect would be started by dropping this pebble in the pond."

"The appointed day for this get-together arrived, and we met at a local hotel conference room. The time flew by," Bill says. "These pastors were sharp. They asked great questions. They had passion for God and their congregations. I was energized by our time together. As I pulled out of the parking lot at the end of that afternoon, I sensed a distinct, two-word whisper from God: *'Serve pastors.'* Just two words. But they resonated in my heart. I said to God, 'If You can use Your activity at Willow Creek and conversations like today's to grow Your kingdom in churches beyond South Barrington, then count me in!' In many ways, this was the launch of Willow Creek's involvement in the global, 'big C' church."

The Global Church Comes Together
By 1989, this initial gathering of pastors had grown to three conferences per year, each with about 500 pastors who came for a time of equipping, encouragement, and worship—and to hear about God's activity through Willow Creek.

THE LOCAL CHURCH IS THE HOPE OF THE WORLD

Since the birth of the Willow Creek Association in 1991, more than 1.5 million church leaders around the world have received WCA training and inspiration, and tens of thousands of churches from more than 90 denominations receive WCA resources. Through live satellite technology, the Leadership Summit is simulcast across North America, and through DVDs the Global Leadership Summit spans the globe, reaching more than 400 cities around the world each year.

The Leadership Summit is the one of the top leadership events of its kind in the world. Gifted, innovative, impactful leaders from a diverse field of expertise gather together every August in South Barrington, Illinois, to challenge church leaders to lead as if lives depended upon it—because they do.

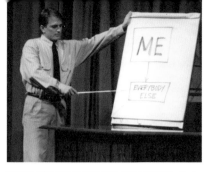

"God used the conferences at Willow to awaken the evangelistic calling in so many churches," says Jim Mellado, president of the Willow Creek Association. "Far too many churches in North America viewed themselves as a place for the 'already convinced.' Reaching out to those who had no relationship with God was someone *else's* job—Young Life's job, or Billy Graham's job, or Campus Crusade's job. Slowly, pastors began to see it as *their* job. They caught the fire of passion for their friends who didn't know Christ, and began to back up their belief that lost people matter to God by prioritizing their budget, staff, and personal relationships toward this end. They refocused their Sunday morning services to create experiences that would be inviting to explorers. They gave up vacation time to attend conferences and grow in their leadership and passion for God. Pastors and leaders understood on the deepest level that they've never locked eyes with someone who doesn't matter to God. And it forever changed them."

"Hosting pastors and leaders from myriad denominations, locations, and backgrounds was a privilege our staff didn't take lightly," Bill says. "They poured their hearts—and countless hours—into serving our conference guests, on top of their regular church-side responsibilities. As conference attendance grew and the number of conferences each year increased, we stepped back to evaluate. First and foremost, *Willow Creek is a church whose mission is to help people far from God become fully devoted followers of Christ*. It became apparent that in order to stay both on-mission to our calling as a church *and* be good stewards of the opportunity for kingdom influence God seemed to be offering, a structural change within Willow was needed."

The Willow Creek Association is Born

At the end of 1991, Willow Creek the church launched Willow Creek the Association—a not-for-profit ministry created to stir up, call out, and equip church leaders to build life-changing Acts 2 churches around the world. A small staff was hired, whose energies, gifts, and passions would be dedicated to helping equip, train, and encourage churches beyond Willow's walls. Unlike many denomination-based, foreign missions organizations that utilize a strategy of establishing new churches under the mantle of their denominational affiliation, the Willow Creek Association (WCA) holds a vision of equipping Christian pastors and leaders in existing churches and community organizations, regardless of their denominational affiliation, for the sole purpose of transforming their communities for Jesus Christ.

Going Global

With a staff focused on serving the global church, the Willow Creek Association nurtured relationships with pastors and community leaders in dozens of countries around the world. Many of these leaders lived in locations and economic circumstances that made attending a South Barrington conference impossible. By taking Willow Creek conferences abroad, the WCA made it possible for these local church leaders, as well as church volunteers, to receive encouragement, equipping, and much-needed training to help their churches prevail.

In response to the groundswell of the Spirit and requests from church leaders, the WCA planned conferences geared toward a variety of areas of ministry: Children and youth ministries, small groups, the arts, women's ministry, a communicator's conference, and more. The global church was hungry for such extensive nourishment.

For nearly a decade this full range of conferences served the global church well. However, it became increasingly clear that in their excitement to catch the wave of the Holy Spirit's activity at Willow, some pastors understandably focused on replicating "the Willow model"—the creativity or methods used in Willow Creek services—in their own churches, anticipating the same results. But what was happening at Willow wasn't spurred by ministry tips or new methods. It was a movement of the Holy Spirit, born of transformed hearts becoming radically devoted to Christ. So in 1995, the WCA launched a new kind of conference, targeted specifically toward the personal and spiritual development of church leaders—a "leadership summit."

Change a Leader, Change a Church

"The Global Leadership Summit acts as a catalyst to ignite a fire inside leaders, to break their hearts toward the things that break the heart of God," says Jim. "The focus isn't about a particular ministry model or strategy; it's about the spiritual transformation of their hearts and the development of their skills. It is about capturing and replicating the Holy Spirit-fueled essence of the early days of Willow, which mirrored the early days of the Acts 2 church. Methods may or may not be transferrable from one setting or culture to the next. But the heart of a leader who is moldable, passionate, and tender toward God crosses all cultural environments and denominational styles. Increasingly, we sensed the importance of putting our full energies toward this type of transformation."

A Collision of Circumstance

"In the past few years," says Jim, "a collision of circumstances affirmed a shift in strategy for the WCA. The significant downturn in the US economy preceded—and perhaps caused—a downturn in attendance at WCA conferences, with the exception of The Leadership Summit (in the US) and The Global Leadership Summit (throughout the world). We assessed this trend and prayerfully considered what shifts God would have the WCA make as it lived out its mission of equipping churches in the days and years to come. This prompted some necessary endings in 2009, as the WCA discontinued its ministry-specific conferences and redirected all energies, staff, and budget toward pouring into church leaders spiritually through the vehicle of The Global Leadership Summit and other church-wide transferable tools.

"In today's ever-changing culture," says Jim, "we must search for *process* solutions, not only *product* solutions, to the challenges church leaders and pastors face. We seek to offer powerful leadership development opportunities for the sake of spiritual transformation through the local church, applicable in any setting, regardless of church method, culture, denomination, or era."

TODAY AND BEYOND

Willow's commitment to being a church that shares *"concern for all the churches,"* as the apostle Paul says in 2 Corinthians 11:28, compels its congregation to serve the global church community.

"We live in a day in which political structures and humanistic morality have failed to bring healing or even relief to our broken world," says Bill. "But there is hope. The local church is the hope of the world. At the end of the day, we are more convinced than ever that the WCA's overarching mission is right on point: Global pastors and leaders are in vital need of the kind of spiritual encouragement and equipping that transcends management styles, cultural mores, or societal trends. Paul challenges believers, 'If God has given you leadership ability, take the responsibility seriously.'[58] God has granted us the opportunity to lead. And the WCA takes this mantle of responsibility and this privilege fully to heart."

CONGO

Sarah Tshiala
Sarah Tshiala Mwamba

All Nations Anglican
Kinshasa,
Congo

THE GLOBAL LEADERSHIP SUMMIT

GLS Partner

06FULLY CONCERNED

06
FULLY CONCERNED
COMPASSION AND JUSTICE

"I am the living testimonial to a weekend message titled, 'All Hands on Deck,'" says Debra.[59] "So many different compassion ministries helped me as a single mom—a seeker struggling to find hope in the midst of divorce, domestic abuse, and financial challenges. Through Divorce Recovery, Oasis, Promiseland, Food Pantry, CARS ministry, Good Sense, and Pastoral Care, my sons and I made the transition from surviving to thriving. Today, we all have been baptized, I serve as a Divorce Recovery coach and speaker, I

Nutritious meals packed by Willow Creek volunteers through Feed My Starving Children rescue 10,000 Zimbabwean children from the brink of starvation.

donated a car back to CARS Ministry, I bought a small townhouse through a grant with the help of Good Sense ministry, both my sons attend college, and after ten years of being single, another leader in Divorce Recovery proposed to me in the chapel and we were married at Willow Creek. Without Willow's wonderful compassion ministries, I might still be without Jesus, trying to make it on my own."

otooo

"Two years ago, after Bill's teaching on God's whispers," says Chris,[60] "I sensed His leading to get involved in the Lake County Jail Ministry, doing Bible study with inmates on Tuesday nights. Four months ago, I met Randy. When he was released from jail, he started attending Willow Creek North Shore. Two weeks ago, I had the awesome privilege of standing waist-deep in the waves of Lake Michigan, holding Randy's young daughter in my arms as he was baptized—a life renewed through the love of Jesus Christ."

otooo

Jackie[61] says, "As the Compassion and Justice Pastor at Willow's North Shore campus, I often witness God's activity in other people's lives. But I had no idea the ride He had in store for me personally: After praying as Bill challenged us to pray, 'God, rock my world,' I pondered how much extra room I had in my two-bedroom condo. God has a sense of humor! I was single and had no experience with kids, but—like many other North Shore families—I opened my home and heart to a pregnant teenager through the Safe Families ministry. I learned lessons in compassion and justice that can only be learned by loving someone in a time of need."

otooo

"I found Willow in 1990 when I was just three years sober from alcoholism," says Jennifer.[62] "Since then, I've been privileged to participate in six international serving trips, volunteer for the food pantry, pray with the local compassion prayer team, serve in the inner city, be challenged by hundreds of messages, and cultivate life-long friendships. When I had an unplanned pregnancy, I received food, diapers, and prayer from the Food Pantry, financial help, a reliable car from CARS ministry, and plenty of love and encouragement. I have been sober now for 23 years, I'm in my last year of grad school, and I am financially independent."

otooo

"When I was a single mom raising my boys," says Mary,[63] "I received so many gifts of help, including a car through the CARS ministry. The compassion shown to me during that season taught me to be always on the lookout for ways I can help others. I still don't have the financial resources to help as much as I'd like, but whenever I can give back, it fills me up!"

"He comforts us in all our troubles so that we can comfort others."

—2 Corinthians 1:4a (NLT)

otooo

Melissa's[64] disabilities don't keep her from spreading God's compassion. "I am 21 years old and doing great, even though I deal with the challenges of a disability. I was 12 when my family began attending Willow. It was a difficult time for me and I was going through a hard depression. God used the Special Friends ministry to help me. Eventually I was blessed to discover I could be a blessing to others. The Lord whispered to me, 'Help a new family with special needs, just like when you were new.' Today, I serve with Special Friends to welcome families with special needs. Willow has been a big help to me and my family."

otooo

"We began coming to Casa de Luz four years ago," says Josefina.[65] "When I was diagnosed with breast cancer one year ago, I faced surgery and painful, debilitating treatments. Jesus Christ came to our family and my life when we needed Him the most. Jesus was always at our side. He was my strong fortress, the motivation I needed to face each chemotherapy session. God used my illness to transform my life. He healed me, body and soul, and I see everything differently now. I have fallen in love with God, the One who gave me life—twice. I am ready to serve others with lots of love because love is what I received from Him. We now host a house group every Friday. My daughters serve in Casa, and my husband Moises helps with the production team. I love reading the Bible, singing praises, and offering words of encouragement to others. Thank you, Lord, for allowing me to go through this experience and helping me realize how much You love me and my family. You are my living breath, the way and the heart of my life. All the glory be to God."

otooo

In addition to Willow ministries serving people facing hardships or poverty within our church and local community, global partnerships with ministries in Latin America and Africa allow us to play a part in providing food, clean water, education, health care, vocational training, HIV/AIDS prevention and care, support for orphans and vulnerable children, micro-enterprise loans, and more to people living in extreme poverty.

"These ministry partners are our heroes," says Warren Beach, director of Willow's Global Connections.

"They spread God's compassion in the harshest of environments and the most challenging of circumstances."

Willow's annual springtime initiative, Celebration of Hope, gives Willow Creek's entire congregation—and the community outside Willow's walls—the opportunity to support these global partners by volunteering time to pack meals or package vegetable seeds for family gardens to be shipped overseas, and by raising funds for other solutions to global poverty.

"I was already interested in issues related to clean water," says Jim,[66] "when I heard Darren [Whitehead]'s message, in which he mentioned how much we Americans spend each year just on ice cream. It rocked me. **I have committed to not eat another bite of ice cream until I have my hands fully involved in getting a well built in a place that needs clean water.**"

otooo

Laura and Matt[67] and their kids have made Celebration of Hope an annual family tradition. "Each spring, we help with the meal or seed packing. The kids understand the impact their efforts make on other children clear around the world in Zimbabwe. This year, we invited the girls' Brownie troop to volunteer with us. Almost everyone came, knowing they were making a true difference in the world, a difference that reflects the heart of God."

otooo

Marg[68] uses her talent as a painter to highlight our calling to compassionate action. "Bill's message, 'Holy Discontent,' prompted me to use my art for God's kingdom," she says. "God led me to begin a company called CompassionArt, which uses creative images and compelling stories to help organizations raise awareness and funds for compassion ministries. One artist named Maria, used her art to raise $4,000 to rebuild a feeding center for poor children in Honduras. And this is just the beginning of what Willow artists hope to do."

oﬔooo

"We were new to Willow Creek during Celebration of Hope 2008," says Yvonne.[69] "This experience helped my sons really understand the power of prayer, compassion, and community. We looked at our weekly budget, and discussed 'needs' versus 'wants.' We cut most items in the 'want' column and put that money toward paying for 800 meal packs for Zimbabwe orphans. We also helped pack the meals and volunteered at the Fair Trade Market. As a family, COH gave us the opportunity to pour out compassion on others. We learned that by God's grace and with great love, all things are possible."

oﬔooo

"Three weeks of disciplined saving, eating, and serving during Celebration of Hope have changed my life!" says John.[70] "In my role as Africa Operations Director at Willow Creek, I am privileged to visit our global partners on a regular basis and see the impact of Celebration of Hope first hand. No longer do I eat a meal without thinking of those who go hungry, or get a glass of water without thinking about the young girl pulled from school—and her future—to fetch water for her family (and unclean water, at that). No longer do I take for granted the blessings God has poured out on me and my family, and no longer do I think that those blessings are just for me. He is giving me the opportunity to grow through living responsibly, giving generously, and loving compassionately."

oﬔooo

"At the start of Celebration of Hope 2008, my wife Anita and I received a Celebration of Hope brochure and read, 'Hunger Has a Name.'" says Frank.[71] "As we read through the initiative, we felt the five-day food challenge would be a great opportunity to better understand hunger. And how hard could it be to just eat rice and beans for a week? But what happened impacted us more than we ever expected. This process gave us the ability to feel the mental and physical anguish that accompanies hunger for millions around the world every day. Our family's involvement in COH '08 led to ongoing involvement in compassion projects in Haiti and the Dominican Republic. As for the 'Hunger Has a Name' brochure...it has been on my desk ever since.

When I look at the photo of six-year-old Murana, it reminds me that hunger not only has a name, but a face, a body, and a soul."

In Santo Domingo, Dominican Republic, thousands of shoe-shine boys, some as young as seven years old, wander the streets day and night, carrying little wooden shoe-shine boxes, looking for a way to make money. Some live in tin shacks; others have no home at all. Perhaps a street vendor or cafeteria owner will offer a bit of leftover food or a tourist will share a few pesos. The boys suffer from the elements, the harsh life on the streets, and malnutrition.

But a Willow Creek partner church in Santo Domingo, Iglesia Comunitaria Cristiana, is reaching out to the shoe-shine boys. Two years ago, the church started a soup kitchen where the boys come each day to receive a healthy meal and loving attention. Iglesia Comunitaria Cristiana has become a refuge of hope for these children, who are growing in height, weight, and self-confidence.

Catherine knows the power of seed in Africa. As the sole breadwinner for her five children—three of them adopted orphans—she is now providing basic needs for her family, thanks to a handful of seeds. Several years ago, Catherine planted a small kitchen garden. Her first crop produced enough to feed her family, with surplus left to sell to the community. The following year, Catherine invested part of her profit ($120 US) in fertilizer and maize seed. The maize she planted on her land—less than an acre—yielded 7,000 pounds of maize! Again she sold the surplus, and was able to buy three more acres with her profits. Catherine's children are now thriving on the fresh corn, beans, and other vegetables in their diet; and because of her family's increased food security and additional income, Catherine now has time to serve as a volunteer care provider, looking after AIDS patients in her community.

There is power in a seed.

Sometimes the most generous gifts come from those who have the least to give. Last year, Pastor Trevor Downham of Norwegian Settler's Church in Durban, South Africa had just received funding to install a borehole well in his community, which would mean fresh, clean water, at last. But while attending a gathering of leaders from Willow partner churches in South Africa, Trevor felt an unsettling nudge from God. When the pastor of neighboring Mdanstane Community Church shared his ministry challenges—which included starting a water-dependent poultry and community garden project—Trevor felt an unmistakable leading to give his church's borehole funding to Mdanstane. So that's what he did!

Today, Mdanstane village is thriving with their new borehole well. Trevor and his church, who gave sacrificially to their neighbors, trusted God to meet their water needs. God enabled those who donated to Willow Creek's Celebration of Hope fund in 2010 to help meet those needs by providing Trevor and his church with funding for a borehole well of their own.

otooo

Association Vida (Patzun, Guatemala Highlands) In 1996, following years of bloody civil war in Guatemala, peace was negotiated between the government and guerrilla forces, and a ministry called Asociacion Vida was launched to provide the people in Patzun with health education, human rights education, and medical care. Today, Asociacion Vida provides medical, dental, and community health education services to more than 20,000 people each year, and its leadership in the community has led to a dramatic decrease in human rights violations. A local church now meets in the medical clinic's multipurpose room, and Asociacion Vida trains and consults with other churches interested in replicating their community outreach model.

otooo

Sobia Network (Ndola, Zambia) Sobia is a network of 26 churches focused on improving the basic living standards of vulnerable widows and orphans. In addition to providing income-generating activities and paying school fees, Sobia offers HIV/AIDS education, water filtration systems, and health and hygiene programs—and serves nutritious meals to 180 households each week!

otooo

Iglesia Nueva Jerusalem (Comecayo, El Salvador) In this small town where gang violence is rampant and most people live on less than $2 a day, New Jerusalem Church is thriving with a weekend attendance of more than 1,000 people—and bringing spiritual, social, and economic transformation to the community of Comecayo.

"For years we've heard that the local church is the hope of the world," says Deanna,[72] a Willow volunteer who recently served in El Salvador."We were able to witness this hope firsthand through the care and compassion delivered through Iglesia Nueva Jerusalem with Willow's support. People are growing in relationship with Christ because this church is committed to partnering with the community to solve the problems resulting from real poverty. The church has helped with home gardens, public schools, public road construction, health and sanitation services, and home construction for the poorest of the poor. Our Salvadoran brothers and sisters send their greetings and gratitude back to the people of Willow Creek. How blessed Willow is to be able to walk alongside this difference-making church and see how we can assist them in transforming their community so that Christ is glorified."

Collin Alto Baptist Church (Vilcun, Chile): When Spain conquered the Americas nearly 500 years ago, they forcefully took control of nearly every mountain, valley, and plain between the southern US and South America. The native Mapuche people of southern Chile have been discriminated against ever since. Subsistence agriculture and migrant fruit-picking jobs are the only options for most Mapuche. But Willow ministry partner Pastor Eleuterio Cayulao at Collin Alto Baptist Church is working with other local churches to change that reality. By starting a jam-making co-op and a community greenhouse, digging wells, and offering adult education and vocational training, churches are giving the Mapuche people the dignity and hope they lost centuries ago.

Red Viva and the International Justice Mission (IJM) Church Network (El Alto, Bolivia High Sierra): On the outskirts of Bolivia's capital city of La Paz at an elevation of over 13,000 feet, lies the city of El Alto. The air is cold and thin, and the land is hard to cultivate, but the promise of a new life in the city continues to draw rural people in and drives meteoric population growth. Such unrestricted growth has created a maze of social problems, including an epidemic of domestic violence and sexual abuse. Safety is in short supply, but Red Viva (The Life Network) and International Justice Mission are working together to network churches and equip leaders to address this crisis. With Willow's partnership, Red Viva and IJM provide after-school programs with nutritious meals, counseling, education in biblical justice and human rights, legal defense for victims of abuse, shelter for abused women and children, vocational training and micro-enterprise development—truly a new life in this city.

otooo

[They] had everything in common. Selling their possessions and goods, they gave to anyone as he had need.   —Acts 2:44b–45

Roman oppression was escalating, and Jewish teachers of the Law spewed hatred at those who claimed Jesus as the Messiah. In the wake of Jesus' trial and crucifixion, no follower was safe. Daily life became treacherous. Midnight raids and arrests were commonplace.

Who would have blamed this little band of Christ followers if they had just circled their wagons and turned inward, keeping their mouths shut and their future secure. They could have faded safely into the pages of history, an isolated sect on the fringe of society who once claimed their Rabbi to be the Son of God.

But grace had happened.

These first-century men and women—Jews, Greeks, slave, and free—had experienced firsthand the unconditional love of God, given through the blood sacrifice of His only Son, their Rabbi Jesus Christ. And when you encounter grace like that, turning inward is not an option. It is a story that must be told. Overwhelmed by the love of God, the early church did what is natural to do in the face of such a love: They turned outward.

All the believers were one in heart and mind. No one claimed that any of his possessions was his own, but they shared everything they had. With great power the apostles continued to testify to the resurrection of the Lord Jesus, and much grace was upon them all. There were no needy persons among them. For from time to time those who owned lands or houses sold them, brought the money from the sales and put it at the apostles' feet, and it was distributed to anyone as he had need.
                                                                —Acts 4:32–35

"In an agricultural society where most people struggled against nature to make ends meet," says Bill Hybels, "and at a time in history when the disparity between rich and poor was viewed as a spiritual judgment, the act

Providing food for those who are hungry has been a long-standing value of Willow Creek.

The CARS ministry's team of volunteer mechanics repair donated cars, providing single parents with reliable transportation.

Displays of Fair Trade products and water systems open peoples' eyes to the variety of ways we can make a difference in the developing world.

"Whatever you did for the least of these…"
Pastors on call listen to peoples' stories, pray with them, and help them determine next steps toward health and wholeness for their circumstance.
Willow Creek's Prison and Jail Ministry reaches out to incarcerated individuals, offering hope, life skills, and the love of Christ.
Every Thursday night from October through April, Willow Creek South Barrington serves as a shelter for homeless individuals through **P.A.D.S.**[72]

Long-term, sustainable food solutions are made possible in Zimbabwe through the 500,000 family packs of vegetable seeds packed by Willow Creek volunteers.

of communal living—providing for one another to ensure all were cared for—was a radical concept. And such radical living and loving caused those around them to take note. No doubt the 'growth engine' of the early church was not just the words of the disciples describing God's love, but the way in which they lived out His love. In fact, these believers earned the nickname, 'the Way,'[74] because they lived in the way of Jesus."

Likewise, over the past 35 years, Christ followers at Willow Creek have sought to live their lives in the way of Jesus, caring for 'anyone as he had need.'

BACK IN THE DAY

"I remember the very day Willow turned a corner in its calling to be a community of compassion in our broken world," says Greg Hawkins, Willow's executive pastor. "It was 1995, and the leadership team was up in Wisconsin on its annual planning retreat. Bill had asked us to go off by ourselves and spend time in prayer listening for God's leading for our church during this next ministry season. When we reconvened, we gathered in a circle and Bill asked, 'Has anyone sensed some direction or leading from God?' Everyone was quiet; even though most of us had been at Willow for a long time, it felt a little intimidating to be the first one to speak about a direct leading from God. But finally, a newer team member stuck his neck out and said, 'I really sense God is calling us to turn our focus outward—away from ourselves—and see if we can be God's hand of blessing to others beyond our walls.'"

"'That's *exactly* what I was sensing,' Bill said. One by one, each of the team members enthusiastically concurred. And in full unity, they decided that out of deep gratitude for God's bountiful blessing on our church, it was time to up the ante in passing that blessing forward."

This vision was shared with Willow's congregation, who affirmed God's leading by contributing around $1.7 million toward this end. A team was assembled to begin planning how to address social concerns of people living in Chicagoland and globally.

For many years—since the theater days, even—individuals in the Willow Creek family had been passing God's blessing forward by providing tangibly for those in need. Early on, one man's observation that a family was going hungry led him to begin bringing bags of groceries in the trunk of his car, to distribute after church on Sundays. This was the beginning of Willow Creek's Care Center and Food Pantry.

By the mid-90s Willow was also engaged in ministry in Latin America. Tom and Dee Yaccino were Willow staff living in the Dominican Republic, serving as liaisons between Willow Creek and our Latin American ministry partners, and hosting teams of volunteers from Willow who traveled to the DR to serve alongside our partners in meeting practical needs in poor communities.

"By 1998, countless individuals in small pockets throughout the church were quietly meeting the physical needs of those in our midst, and beyond," says Heather Larson, Willow Creek's director of Compassion and Justice. Hundreds of volunteers were committed to ongoing service to our Latin American partners, and Extension ministry—Willow's ministry to those fighting poverty locally—was launched that year, so thousands of Willow Creek volunteers began serving downtown Chicago and in other local communities. Axis, our 18 to 20-something ministry, was focusing its ministry vision on developing a culture of compassion and serving, and became deeply engaged in local and global engagement. But the people involved in these ministries were scattered throughout Willow in isolated pockets. They were doing cool, radical things, but their vision was not yet woven into the Willow culture.

"It really wasn't until 2003, when Lynne Hybels and several Willow staff members witnessed firsthand the tragedy of extreme poverty and AIDS in Africa," Heather says, "that issues of compassion and justice began to rise to the surface of our church as a whole."

In 2004, at Lynne's prompting, Bill Hybels took a trip to Samfya, an isolated community in rural Zambia, and his eyes were opened to the reality of a problem so tragic and so huge, he knew it would take our entire church to make a difference.

"The trip to Samfya was a déjà vu experience in many ways," says Bill. "God had first tugged on my heart about the plight of those living in extreme poverty when I was 16 years old and my admittedly eccentric father decided it was time for me to expand my worldview. I found myself traveling alone throughout Scandinavia, to the Middle East, and then headed for Nairobi, Kenya. On a bustling dirt road in that poverty riddled city, I saw a level of human suffering I hadn't known existed. A boy my age held out a tin cup to me, balanced on what was left of his leprosy eaten arm. Our eyes locked, and he uttered a single word: 'Penny?' All I had in my pocket was an American

Express card—useless to him. 'Sorry,' I shrugged, and embarrassed, I turned away. I rushed back to my hotel room, fell to my knees, and wept. Even though I had little relationship with God at that point in my life, I poured my heart out to Him. And I heard His inaudible whisper in response: 'If you will allow me to guide your life, one day I will use you to relieve some of the pain you see.'

"Sitting on a dirt floor in Samfya three decades later," Bill says, "this whispered conversation from my teens came flooding back to me. 'Now is the day,' I sensed God saying. I knew He was guiding us as a church to put our hand to the plow against the kind of poverty and human suffering I was witnessing once again."

"We began to understand as a church that there are huge needs in our world that break the heart of God—needs that we could do something about," says Heather. "Until this time, issues of compassion and justice had gripped the hearts of a few 'radicals' in the church, but now it was becoming a church-wide thing, something that Bill and the other teachers talked about from talked about at weekend services, something everyone in the congregation was being invited to get involved in."

Becoming Invisible

The ministry approach Willow followed in Africa was based on the pattern Tom and Dee Yaccino had established earlier in Latin America. Rather than pouring ourselves into large, international charities (NGOs—non-government organizations) or adopting a traditional missions approach in which a church establishes its own ministries or plants new churches in distant countries, Willow adopted a partnership model. Tapping into the Yaccinos' educational expertise and past experience in Latin American culture, Willow's global engagement was built upon a foundation of relationships, networks, and partnerships with the *real* experts in Latin America—the local Latin American pastors and community leaders themselves.

"Since that time, our strategy has been one of becoming invisible," says Heather, "of working behind the scenes to support existing local efforts in Latin America and in Africa."

Warren Beach (a long-time Willow member and husband to Nancy), was one of the first "radicals" involved in Willow's Latin American partnerships. When it became apparent that God was leading toward engagement in Africa, Warren left his position in the marketplace to become a full-time volunteer, leading Willow's aligned global efforts in Latin America and Africa as director of Global Connections.

"Our goal is to keep developing great relationships with those on the front lines of the battle against HIV/AIDS and extreme poverty," Heather says. "We want to build more partnerships, both in the number of churches and the depth of our relationships with them, so we can see God transform their communities—and our hearts. We need those who are poor just as much as they need us. We experience God differently when we open up our hearts to others. Our dream is to see God's compassionate heartbeat woven deeply into our congregation, that we would be living out the values of compassion and justice, both corporately and individually."

THROUGH THE YEARS
A Celebration of Hope

In order to help capture the hearts of the entire church for the plight of global brothers and sisters living in poverty, the Compassion and Justice team knew the congregation needed hands-on involvement. In response to specific needs from Willow's global partners, Compassion and Justice sponsored a gifts-in-kind drive in 2007, in which the congregation was invited to donate gently used clothing and household items to be shipped overseas to our ministry partners in Latin America and Africa. The church's overwhelming response filled 18 shipping containers! The following spring, Regifting Depots (reverse garage sales) collected similar items in neighborhoods throughout Willow Creek's footprint.

By 2008, Celebration of Hope had become a springtime Willow tradition. Targeting the issue of global hunger, Willow Creek partnered with Feed My Starving Children (FMSC), a non-profit organization that provides a nutritious rice-based food mixture that church volunteers can pack and ship overseas for children facing extreme malnutrition. More than 14,000 volunteers packed 3.6 million meals during Celebration of Hope 2008, and Willow Creek sent enough meals to Zimbabwe to feed 10,000 children for an entire year. In addition, donations from Willow Creek individuals and families funded long-term solutions to poverty such as micro-enterprise loans, educational opportunities, and job-creating initiatives.

In 2009, Celebration of Hope added the issue of clean water to its spring meal-packing campaign.

"Inaccessibility to clean water cripples entire communities in two ways," says Heather. "Every day, more than 24,000 children in developing countries die from preventable water-borne illnesses as a direct result of drinking contaminated water.[75] In addition, lack of nearby water has a devastating generational effect on young girls, as hauling water is viewed culturally to be the role of women. Girls are often unable to attend school because they must walk several miles multiple times per day to haul water for their families. The resulting lack of education perpetuates poverty as generations of young women cannot better themselves through education or jobs."

In addition to the more than 4 million FMSC meals packed during Celebration of Hope 2009, financial donations enabled the purchase of 28 clean water systems and 106 wells/bore holes in Latin America and Africa, providing drinking water for more than 200,000 people.

When spring 2010 rolled around, Compassion and Justice team members spoke with church leaders from the Zimbabwean villages that had received Willow Creek meal packs. In the previous two years, they had experienced much-needed relief from crippling hunger and malnutrition.

"But as we look to the future," the Zimbabwean leaders said "we want to stabilize our communities through *renewable* food programs. Could you provide vegetable seeds so families can grow their own food?"

In response to this request, Willow's eager hands shifted from meal-packing to seed-packing, as Celebration of Hope volunteers helped entire villages move from emergency food relief to sustainable food provision. Willow families packed enough vegetable seeds for 500,000 family gardens, providing sustainable food and a source of income for families, and a sense of pride and self-sufficiency for entire communities.

"Willow's overwhelming response to our Celebration of Hope projects has infused a deep level of ownership throughout the hearts of our entire congregation," says Heather. "We as a church have realized we truly can make a difference. While it seems like issues of global poverty are insurmountable, we really can make an impact when we all work together."

Christmas Gifts

In addition to springtime Celebration of Hope campaigns that focus on global needs, Willow Creek has developed a tradition of Christmastime giving that focuses on injustice and poverty needs at home in the Chicago area. Christmas giving has helped to stock the shelves of local food pantries—hit particularly hard during the economic downturn. And recent clothing and coat drives have provided new winter gear for more than 10,000 children throughout the Chicago area.

"Christmas is a time when each of us becomes more acutely aware of the tremendous gift God has given us through the birth of His Son Jesus," Heather says. "It's a time of year when people want to give back. And giving to those in need in our community has been a tangible way our congregation can express its gratitude for all God has given us."

On the Home Front
Following the same model of engagement used in Latin America and Africa, Willow's local compassion ministry focuses on building partnerships with community organizations committed to bringing God's love and His tangible care to people facing poverty and injustice throughout the Chicago area.

By serving with these local partners, Willow volunteers have the opportunity to address the needs of people who are homeless, imprisoned, elderly, and facing physical or developmental challenges; children at risk; refugees and immigrants; women facing unplanned pregnancies, and the full range of social issues related to urban poverty.

"We continue to ask ourselves, 'What is happening locally?' Heather says. "Are we responding compassionately and holistically to the needs in our own backyard?"

Willow Creek's attention to the church's neighborhoods goes beyond its economic challenges. The birth of Casa de Luz, Willow Creek's Spanish-speaking community, is a direct result of increased focus on those struggling with language barriers and the integration into a new culture.

A House of Light
In 2006, Hector Hermosillo and his family moved from Mexico to Illinois, in order to pastor Willow Creek's Spanish-speaking congregation, Casa de Luz, which means House of Light. Hector's dream is that God would use Casa de Luz to bring the light of Christ to the thousands of Spanish-speaking people in the neighborhoods surrounding Willow.

"I was the most unlikely of candidates," Hector says. "I didn't bring a deep résumé of strategic planning, and I certainly didn't bring the bilingual skills the hiring team was looking for! At the time, I spoke very little English. But I have a deep passion for this community and a burden for reaching my Spanish-speaking brothers and sisters for Jesus Christ. By God's grace, the team offered me the job, and I accepted."

The core members of Casa de Luz have grown to more than 700 members. In keeping with the highly relational culture of the Hispanic community, Casa builds its congregation on a foundation of one-on-one relationships, family friendships, social activities, and small groups.

"Many of our Casa brothers and sisters are separated from their family, who live in Mexico, or Central or South America," Hector says. "They are isolated from their own culture, and are struggling to adapt to life in America. Casa has become family to them—a big, vibrant, welcoming family. The Casa community helps fill the void in their lives—relationally and spiritually—and helps build a bridge to their new but 'foreign' American culture."

"Being an immigrant is not a distant concept for many of us at Willow," says Bill. "My grandfather was an immigrant from Holland, and I remember well the stories I heard of his own struggles to adjust to American life. Many of us can look back only a generation or two and find our family histories are quite similar to those of our Casa families. It is only natural that the church be a bridge-building agent that spans cultural and language barriers. The Casa community has brought to Willow a new level of understanding and compassion. It has given us a front-row seat to the cultural and socio-economic struggles experienced by many in our Hispanic community. Just as the early church extended itself to both Jew and Greek, we too are called to extend ourselves beyond our cultural comfort zones. And as we do so, we are blessed and enriched."

Welcoming the Stranger

As Willow Creek's understanding of the many challenges facing our Casa family expands, Willow finds itself wrestling with yet another extremely complicated issue: the need for comprehensive immigration reform.

"Many of our Casa de Luz brothers or sisters are directly affected by the complex issue of immigration in the United States," says Bill. "Many have friends or relatives who are undocumented workers who came to America to escape crippling poverty in their own countries. Others face these challenges themselves. These are our brothers and sisters in Christ, members of our congregation. We did not seek out this issue. But it has landed in our laps because it directly affects our Casa family. Scripture speaks clearly about how God's people are to respond to 'strangers'—literally called 'aliens'—in their midst.

The alien living with you must be treated as one of your native-born. Love him as yourself, for you were aliens in Egypt. **—Leviticus 19:34**

"Today, we are wrestling as a leadership team and as a church to determine how we can best help alleviate the suffering caused by an immigration system that both sides of the political aisle agree is not working. As with similar justice issues Willow Creek has faced over the years—the role of women in ministry, racial reconciliation, global poverty, HIV/AIDS—immigration reform is an opportunity to 'release the chains of oppression' as Isaiah's words challenge us to do. As we did with each of those earlier issues that felt insurmountable at the time—and with any issues God may call us to address in the future—we will earnestly seek an understanding of Scripture and listen for God's leading as to how we should respond."

"My dream for Willow Creek," says Hector, "is that we grow as one church, a blending of two rich cultures. It is easy to make assumptions about one another without really knowing each other, to be complacent in an 'us/them' mindset. But we are one church, one body. Come to a Casa service! (We offer Spanish-to-English translation headsets!) Because we have two diverse congregations, we have the privilege of learning from one another and loving one another, just as the early church loved one another in spite of their cultural and language differences."

Is not this the kind of fasting I have chosen: to loose the chains of injustice and untie the cords of the yoke, to set the oppressed free and break every yoke? Is it not to share your food with the hungry and to provide the poor wanderer with shelter—when you see the naked, to clothe him, and not to turn away from your own flesh and blood? If you spend yourselves in behalf of the hungry and satisfy the needs of the oppressed, then your light will rise in the darkness, and your night will become like the noonday.

—Isaiah 58:6–7, 10

TODAY AND BEYOND

With growing clarity and commitment to being God's hands of compassion to our neighbors, Willow Creek leadership is looking forward to a future of increasing local engagement. As a result of a long process of prayerful discernment, the Willow Creek board of Elders and staff are initiating a strategic plan to create a more holistic, Christ-centered ministry to people in our church community and local neighborhoods who are facing the challenges of poverty.

Currently the CARS ministry—a ministry that serves many struggling families by providing reliable transportation—is housed in a specialized facility for auto repair that is located 20 minutes away from Willow's central campus in South Barrington, Illinois. And the Willow Creek Care Center—the largest food pantry in Cook County, Illinois, distributing more than 1.8 million pounds of food last year—is located in a warehouse several miles away from the church. To maximize Willow's ability to provide holistic care, these two key compassion ministries will be relocated to the South Barrington campus.

"By bringing all compassion ministries onto the central campus," says Bill, "we will frame one front door to serve as a welcoming entry point for our neighbors struggling with poverty. Willow Creek will become a holistic facility of hope, providing assistance for immediate needs such as food, housing, transportation, and clothing. In addition, we are expanding to create long-term solutions to those seeking to move themselves out of the cycle of poverty: help with employment, education, recovery from addiction, medical/dental care, and lega/financial advice. **We seek to build a bridge to our neighbors in need.** Having all of these ministries integrated at our South Barrington campus will allow Willow attendees to get more personally involved with compassion ministries, and will allow guests receiving assistance to more clearly see the connection between the tangible expressions of love they are experiencing and the intangible but very real God, from whom this love flows."

"The big-picture plan for this on-site care center is to provide both immediate and long-term assistance," says Executive Pastor Greg Hawkins. "We are not the be-all, end-all solution to peoples' problems, but we can form a great network with other care organizations within our community. We can help those motivated to take next steps on their own journey toward stability and independence—and most of all, toward spiritual transformation."

"We are excited beyond words at the potential of this endeavor," says Heather. "Jesus' words in John 10:10 cast a vision for what life can be like: *'I have come that they may have life, and have it to the full.'* This is our heartbeat. What a privilege to play a role in helping people experience the life Jesus intends for His followers: 'Life to the full.'"

"For 35 years, God has graciously blessed Willow Creek in ways that defy human understanding," Bill says. "With such blessing comes equal responsibility. Jesus cared for people holistically, addressing not just their *spiritual* well-being, but also their physical, social, and economic well-being. As His followers, we are called to do no less. Jesus challenges us with these words:

From everyone who has been given much, much will be demanded; and from the one who has been entrusted with much, much more will be asked.
—Luke 12:48b

"Let's not take these words lightly," says Bill. "God is asking us to give back out of the abundant blessing He's given us. He's offering us the thrill of spending our lives as difference makers in this world. Our God is a God of compassion. His heart is broken by the pain of His people, and He wants our hearts to be broken too—broken to the point that we are moved to *action*, that we are moved to be His hands of healing and help and hope.

"Jesus underscored the call to compassionate action when he said, *'Whatever you did for one of the least of these brothers of mine, you did for me.'* By feeding and clothing and loving people, we are feeding and clothing and loving Jesus Himself. We are honoring His passion, His life, and His sacrificial love.

"**By giving of ourselves as the Acts 2 believers did—by sharing everything we have, and 'giving to anyone as he has need'—we are living out our true identity as the church of Jesus Christ.** I don't know about you, but I can't imagine a more worthy or fulfilling way to spend my days."

07 FOREVER DEVOTED

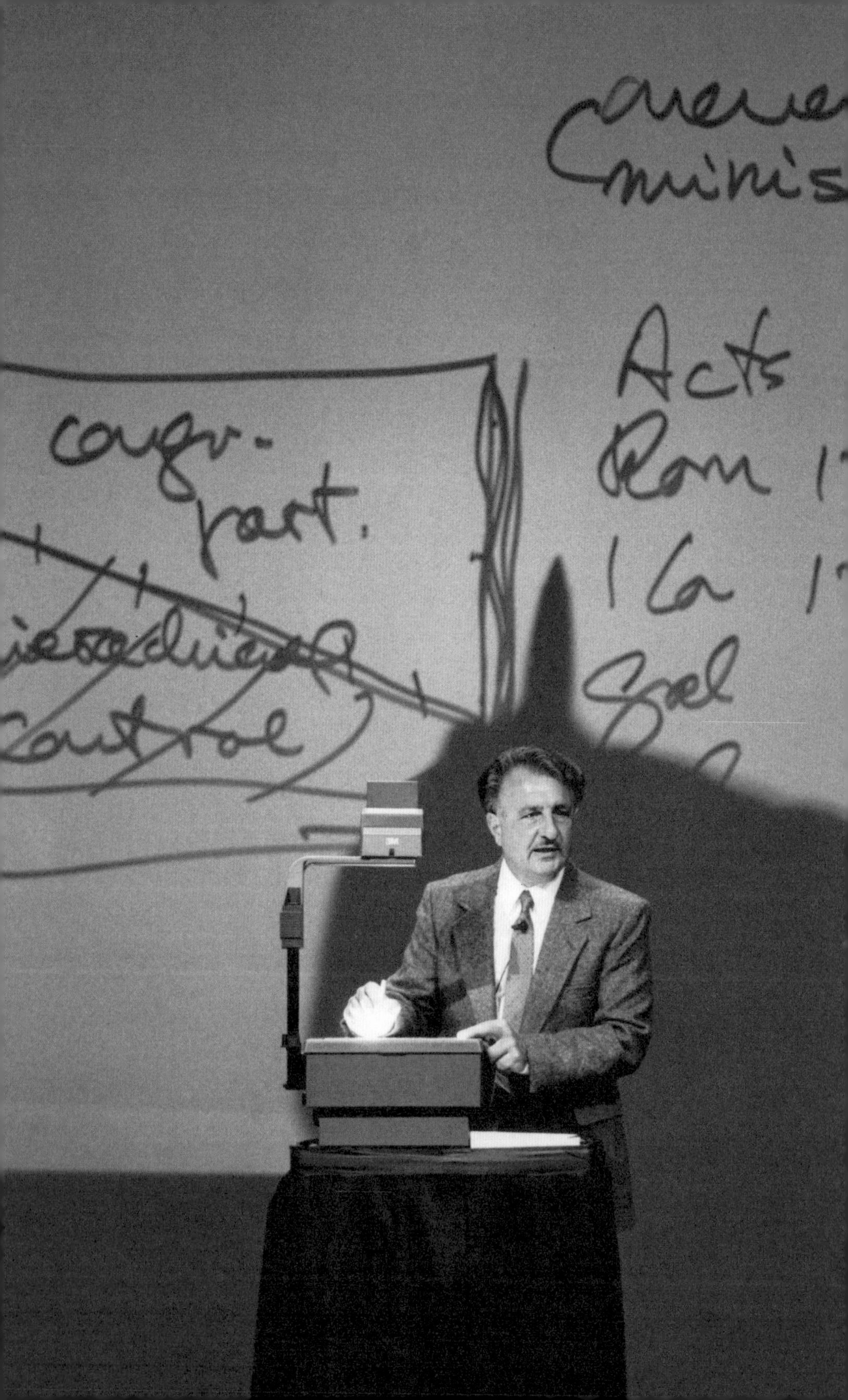
cong.
part.
Acts

FOREVER DEVOTED
TURNING THE PAGE

"Swear to never repeat what I am about to tell you," the man in the expensive suit said to Dr. Gilbert Bilezikian after waiting for a word in private at the close of Dr. B's Willow Creek message.

Dr. B has agreed to keep this vow for nearly three decades, but changed circumstances allow him to tell this man's story now:

"'I had all the money I wanted,' the man said. 'I had a beautiful family, a big house in the suburbs and an apartment on the Gold Coast, a boat on Lake Michigan, foreign sports cars. But because of you people, I lost everything. My wife and two daughters are in hiding somewhere in the United Kingdom. I live in a little studio apartment under a false identity, and I work as a box carrier in a publishing house. I've lost everything, and it's your fault.'

"I was deeply moved by his story. 'I am sorry for your hardship,' I told the man, 'but help me understand how it is the church's fault?' He explained.

"As a high-ranking leader in a mob family, I was in charge of drugs and prostitution in our section of Chicago," he said. "One day, one of my girlfriends asked me to promise to do her a favor. 'Sure,' I said, thinking she would ask for a gift. But instead, she asked me to go to a new kind of church with her. Because a promise is binding in the mob, I came with her to Willow Creek.

"The 'show' meant nothing to me, and the 'speech' sounded like utter nonsense. But I was captivated by the behavior of the people. They greeted each other with obvious joy, and hung around after the service as if they didn't want to leave. I watched the 'guides' welcome people, and saw how the staff and people on stage related to each other. In our organization, we know what family is. But I had never seen family like this. I could tell it was real.

"I came back the next Sunday, alone this time. I became hooked, watching Christian 'community' happen. I just kept coming back, watching.

"Eventually the messages began to make sense, and I realized I was sinful and in need of a Savior. One Sunday, I quietly turned my life over to Jesus. Soon after, I went to the Feds to confess my 'family activity' and to make restitution. As a result, I lost everything. I'm now under federal protection. But please, don't feel bad for me. If I had lost a thousand times as much, I would gladly give it all up for what God has given me now.

"In the coming years," says Dr. B, "I would see this man in the Sunday crowd. We would discreetly acknowledge each other from a distance. Then, suddenly, he disappeared. I never saw him again. I eventually accepted that either he had joined his family in a distant country, or perhaps the long, murderous tentacles of the mob had at last caught up him and wreaked revenge.

"This brother without a name came to faith in Christ and was won for eternity, not because of the quality of our services or the power of our preaching, but rather—like those drawn to the warm center of Christian love that marked the first century church—this brother was drawn to Christ simply by seeing the example of Willow's family living out its calling as an authentic, biblical community."

BACK IN THE DAY

"In a college classroom more than 35 years ago," Dr. B reflects, "something ignited between a young Midwestern American college student with a bright business future ahead of him and the heavily academic teaching of an accented European moss-back scholar. The student, Bill Hybels, was free-spirited, adventurous, and risk-taking. By the time he became a college student, he was already adept at various sports—sailing, flying, racing cars, and motorcycling across the country. I—the professor—was a little bookish man, raising a family of four lively young children, and whose idea of adventure was to escape to a college library carrel.

"But between this unlikely pair, a life-changing connection was established. Bill responded radically to a teaching that did not even stir his classmates from their blissful somnolence. He caught the vision of the Acts 2 church that had captured me years earlier, and he ran with it. With God guiding our human efforts, through the years we have earnestly sought to build the community of oneness we see reflected in Acts 2.

They devoted themselves to the apostles' teaching and to the fellowship, to the breaking of bread and to prayer. Everyone was filled with awe, and many wonders and miraculous signs were done by the apostles. All the believers were together and had everything in common. Selling their possessions and goods, they gave to anyone as he had need. Every day they continued to meet together in the temple courts. They broke bread in their homes and ate together with glad and sincere hearts, praising God and enjoying the favor of all the people. And the Lord added to their number daily those who were being saved. —Acts 2:42–47

An Inner Call

"Since the day I surrendered my life to Jesus Christ as a 17-year-old at a Christian camp in Wisconsin," says Bill Hybels, "I sensed deep in my soul an unspoken longing for the kind of community described in these verses in Acts. I didn't have the words to put around them at the time; it wasn't until years later in Dr. B's college classroom that the vision of the Acts 2 church struck home and I was able to put a label on the longing I felt. But feel it I did—to the core of my being! And I think I am no different from anyone else. I believe we all have a 'homing sensor,' a magnetic pull that draws us toward community.

"Since Creation, the deepest needs of human beings have remained unchanged," says Bill. "People at their core are love-starved; they're purpose-starved. 'God has set eternity in the hearts of humankind,'[76] so people wonder about life beyond this world. These core needs are the same across centuries, borders, and cultures. In our society, where external needs are easily met, people can get lulled into the belief that they don't need God, they don't need the church, they don't need friends. Then pain comes their way—as it eventually does in all our lives—and their core needs get exposed. Pain is the great equalizer.

"And the body of Christ—Jesus as the Head and a community of Christians— is the antidote to pain. It's the answer to our inner longings and unmet needs. When tragedy or trials come, authentic Christian community doesn't inoculate us against their pain, but it is the healing balm that provides strength and helps us through. In community we find love. In community we find purpose. We find relationships with God and friends and family, relationships that will span eternity. When the church is working right—when people are doing life together in authentic relationship with one another, celebrating and grieving together, worshiping and serving God together, and together being gradually transformed into the image of Christ—there is nothing more powerful or beautiful to behold. The local church is truly the hope of the world."

FORKS IN THE ROAD

Over the past 35 years the Willow Creek community has faced numerous decision points—major forks in the road—that had to be prayerfully and earnestly navigated in order to discern the course God intended for the church. It wasn't always easy to navigate the theological and relational complexities of these decisions, but in hindsight the grace and guidance of God are abundantly clear.

In the earliest days of Willow, the church's Elders wrestled with the controversial issue of women in leadership. Was it biblical for women to have leadership positions in the church? Could they exercise—as men do—the full range of God-given spiritual gifts? For nearly two years the Elders studied God's Word on this subject. In the end, they concluded that the Bible affirms that God calls and empowers both men and women to lead and teach in the church to the extent that their faith, experience, and character support. For more than three decades, Willow's congregation has benefitted from the prayerful decision made at this critical intersection.

In 1981, when the community left the theatre days behind and moved into
a church home of its own at 67 East Algonquin Road in Barrington, Illinois,
people looking at Willow from the outside saw thousands of people with—by
appearances, at least—plenty of money to spare, moving into an unnecessarily
big and beautiful facility. What they didn't see was the true story of the committed Willow families and individuals who were so convinced that God was
calling them to establish a permanent home that they stood in line together
one Tuesday morning and took out personal bank loans to pay for the land on
which to build. Buying this land was a fork in the road. Those who had been
at Willow from the beginning knew they were viewed by many in the local
community as a fly-by-night group of youthful fanatics. The Willow Elders
believed the church needed to establish itself firmly—and visibly—in this
community if it wanted to be taken seriously as a place where young families seeking God and a place to belong would feel confident to bring their
kids. But was the Willow community ready to pay the price? to literally put
our money on the line? To commit themselves long term to the work they
believed God wanted to do through Willow? Or would they back down from
the challenge, play it safe, and limit themselves from what God could do?

"For the 237 of us standing in line for bank loans that day, it seemed obvious,"
says Bill. "At this fork in the road, we *had* to take this step. It was clearly the
choice God was asking us to make. And in the years since, He has affirmed
this decision over and over again."

Another fork in the road led to Willow's investment in church leaders throughout the world through the Willow Creek Association. Willow staff and church
members said yes to picking up a serving towel and encouraging, supporting,
and equipping church leaders who have come to Willow Creek for ministry
conferences and leadership training. No one could have predicted the joy and
energy this choice would produce in the Willow community.

"Our increasing connection with the global church has brought more personal
joy and fulfillment than I could have imagined," says Bill. "How deeply I resonate with the apostle Paul's reference in 2 Corinthians 11:28 to his *'concern
for all the churches.'* I'm so grateful that God clearly led us down this path."

During the last decade, Willow has faced crossroads in response to global
poverty, HIV/AIDS, racial reconciliation, and most recently, immigration
reform. In the coming months the church will face another fork in the road

as individuals and the congregation as a whole commit their prayers, time, and resources to the new Care Center that will offer hope to so many families in Willow's community.

At each fork in the road, when those in the Willow community have sought God's direction and followed His leading, they have found Him to be faithful to accomplish His purposes through their frail, but earnest efforts.

AS WE TURN THE PAGE

"As I reflect on the stories God has been writing in our church and in my life as a Christ follower," says Bill, "I can't help but recall a conversation I had shortly after I became a Christian. This one conversation in many ways changed my heart, my goals, and my future. An older Christian man took me to dinner and asked me, 'What are you doing with your life that *matters*? What are you doing that will last forever?' Until that point, I hadn't seriously considered that there was anything more significant in life than a decent job and a healthy dose of pleasure. But his words rattled me and caused me to ask questions, not only about my eternal future but also about how I live every day. Even today, every morning when I roll out of bed and my knees hit the floor, I ask God, 'How would You have me spend this day? What do You want me to do that will last forever?'"

"In the closing pages of this book, I issue you the same challenge that rattled my life so many years ago: **What are you doing that will last forever?** How are you spending your one and only life? Are you surrendering each day to God's purposes? Are you chin-deep in authentic, biblical community? Being the church to one another is antithetical to the world's version of success. It's not about might and power and strength. It's about surrender, about becoming less than, about becoming a small part of something much bigger than any individual. It's realizing at the end of the day that all we have—and all we are—is a gift from God.

"What's holding you back? Find a community of people you can do life with. Move forward on your spiritual journey. Take a class. Join a recovery group. Be faithful in meeting together with your church family when it gathers. Volunteer to use your spiritual gifts in service to others. Live out your true identity as a fully devoted follower of Christ. It's an identity you were created for. It's a life you will never regret.

"So, what are you waiting for? Hand God the pen and invite Him to write His story through your life!"

NOTES

Chapter One

1. Matthew 6:10

2. Acts 3–4

3. Acts 7

4. Hebrews 11–12:1

5. Reveal™ is an ongoing study of more than 280,000 in-depth responses from congregants in 1,200 churches across a wide variety of denominations, which helps churches evaluate and implement strategies to help their people grow spiritually. For more information, go to willowcreek.com/reveal.

Chapter Two

6. Donna Simale, Schaumburg, Illinois

7. Tony and Kimberly DeLeo, Gilberts, Illinois

8. Allison will be serving in a closed country and her name has been changed for security reasons.

9. Krista Budzisz, Palatine, Illinois

10. Sandy (last name withheld)

11. "Michelle" (name changed to protect privacy)

12. Andy Martin, Bartlett, Illinois

13. Deb Krich Lacy, Cary, Illinois

14. José Fidel and Maribel Castañeda, Lake Zurich, Illinois

15. *Rediscovering Church*, by Lynne and Bill Hybels, Grand Rapids: Zondervan, 1995, p. 29

16. "Two Hands," by Tom Coomes/Chuck Butler, 1970

17. *Rediscovering Church*, by Lynne and Bill Hybels, Grand Rapids: Zondervan, 1995, p. 33

Chapter Three

18. Brad Amadeo, Gilberts, Illinois

19. Barbara Luecht, Carpentersville, Illinois

20. Patricia McFarland, Huntley, Illinois

21. Lisa Hartell, Lakewood, Illinois

22. Linda B., Naperville, Illinois

23. Lee Zilligen, Palatine, Illinois

24. Debbie Spink, Elgin, Illinois

25. Anthony Eppolito, Algonquin, Illinois

26. Anthony's mentors are Joel Jager, Tom Vitacco, and Ron Ercoli

27. Kym McNabney, Northwest Suburbs of Chicago

28. Bruce Lacy, Cary, Illinois

29. *Rediscovering Church*, by Lynne and Bill Hybels, Grand Rapids: Zondervan, 1995, p. 33

30. Archived message CDs and DVDs are available at Seeds Bookstore on Willow Creek's central campus in South Barrington and smaller branches at each Willow Creek campus. *willowcreek.org/seeds*

31. The first four books of the New Testament in the Bible—the gospels of Matthew, Mark, Luke, and John—each contain narrative accounts of Jesus' life on earth. The gospels were written by eyewitnesses who saw Him teach, interact with people, heal people, extend compassion, and eventually be crucified and resurrected.

Chapter Four

32. Karen and Phil Berndt, Bartlett, Illinois

33. Mike Gillette, Bartlett, IL

34. Aiko Yamada, Evanston, Illinois

35. Theresa (name changed to protect privacy)

36. Catherine Mazanowicz, Palatine, Illinois

37. Donna Watson, Palatine, Illinois

38. Kathryn (name changed to protect privacy)

39. Steve Hamer, Grayslake, Illinois

40. Tara VanderSande, West Dundee, Illinois

41. Vicki Voss, Streamwood, Illinois

42. Robbie and Gary Casten, Wauconda, Illinois

43. John 13:23, John 19:26, and John 21:7, 20

Chapter Five

44. Rony Madrid, Guatemala

45. Sandy McConkey, Spokane, Washington

46. Michael Ryan, Wheaton, Illinois

47. Philip Tutu, Ghana

48. Leanne Davie, Auckland, New Zealand

49. Edwin Colon, Brooklyn, New York

50. Jim and Josh Danielson, Aurora, Illinois

51. Oscar Zamora, Peru

52. Fernando Ley, Quito, Ecuador

53. Fady Eldeiry, Egypt

54. Julian Foe, Indonesia

55. Graeme Paris, United Kingdom

56. Cedrick Mwungu, Democratic Republic of Congo (name changed for security purposes)

57. Gelu Paul-Faina, Romania

58. Romans 12:8b (NLT)

Chapter Six

59. Debra Krich Lacy, Cary, Illinois

60. Chris Tara, lake Bluff, Illinois

61. Jackie Herron-Whitfield, Northbrook, Illinois

62. Jennifer L. Taylor, Hoffman Estates, Illinois

63. Mary Lausche, Crystal Lake, Illinois

64. Melissa Erickson, Palatine, Illinois

65. Josefina Garcia, Hanover Park, Illinois

66. Jim Harding, Streamwood, Illinois

67. Laura and Matt Birk, Palatine, Illinois

68. Marg Rehnburg (for more information on CompassionArt, go to cocmpassionart.us)

69. Yvonne, Andrew, and Colin McLaughlin, Burlington, Wisconsin

70. John Forbes, West Dundee, Illinois

71. Frank Davis, Prospect Heights, Illinois

72. Deanna Hanks, Winnetka, Illinois

73. Public Action to Deliver Shelter, Inc., is an inter-faith program providing shelter and supportive services to homeless persons.

74. Acts 9:2; Acts 19:9, 23; Acts 24:14, 22

75. Statistics provided from water.org

Chapter Seven

76. Ecclesiastes 3:11